Wicked Rich
The Adventures of a Mad Lottery Winner
A Memoir
© 2018 Paula Moore
All Rights Reserved

Wicked Rich

The Adventures of a Mad Lottery Winner

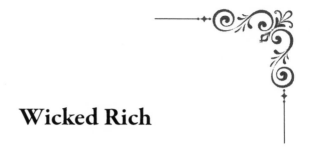

Dedication

All my life, I longed for a sister - someone I could tell my deepest, darkest secrets to. I never was very close to anyone as I grew up, and I never met anyone around whom I was truly and securely myself.
Then ten years ago, I met a remarkable woman named Doti.
Thank you, Doti, for supporting me, for making me laugh, and for keeping my secrets. For accepting me as I am and loving me right where I stand. My life's most enduring comfort is in knowing that no matter what, we are always connected through love.
Thank you for being the sister I thought I'd never have.

"The biggest mistake we can make is trying to force ourselves to be accepted by the world. The mirage of inclusion is perhaps the most powerful lure into a life of subservient futility." - Paula Moore

Foreword

by David Ropeik

I DIDN'T REALIZE THE most valuable thing I had as a local TV reporter, until I left that career to start a new one. As a teacher and communications officer at the Harvard School of Public Health, I found myself among colleagues who were exceptionally intelligent, more engaged in high level thinking about high level national and global health issues than anyone I had ever been with, and both challenging and elevating to be among. But they weren't...well...real. Or maybe it's more fair to say they were only one narrow slice of what people are really like.

The first thing that brought this to my attention was the humor. There wasn't much, and what there was was constrained by all sorts of unspoken but firm limits on anything that even hinted at sexuality, 'ribald' language, or carried the slightest whiff of cultural innuendo. But it wasn't that the jokes weren't at least a little racy. Plenty of great humor is funny without being offensive. It's that, mostly, everybody was so serious. There just wasn't much joking around at all.

Then I noticed there was less talk about local affairs, about local sports, about local politics and government. And there seemed to be a narrower range of how people dressed, how they spoke, what their personal interests were. These qualities weren't bad. I knew that they were just the norms of academia, the new and narrower tribe I was now a part of. But they weren't the norms in the world I was used to, the real and diverse world in which I had traveled as a street reporter for the last 22 years.

I had been all over New England, meeting different kinds of people, in different kinds of circumstances, every day. The rich and the poor and everyone in between. Presidents and priests and prisoners. Firefighters and bus drivers and city clerks. Cops and cabbies and CEOS and politicians and nurses and professional athletes. People celebrating achievements or grieving losses, angry people throwing rocks in street riots or meditatively praying at sacred ceremonies, frightened people struggling in hospital beds to stay alive, homeless people living on the street. Young, old, of every race and cultural and educational background and social and economic class, in all sorts of neighborhoods and homes and offices and workplaces, going through every imaginable human experience and emotion, people with every imaginable set of values and opinions. My press pass, I realized in retrospect, had been an entry ticket to the full wide world. A true gift.

And looking back, I realized the faith this education had given me in the basic decency of most people. It didn't matter where they lived or what they did or how educated they were. It didn't matter what religion or national background they identified with. It didn't much how much money they had. I mean, sure, all those things mattered, shaping how those people were living their lives and interacting with the world. But across all these endless variables, people seemed to share the same basic goals: to stay safe and healthy, get a little further ahead if they could, take care of their kids and families, and treat other people with courtesy.

They seemed to share common values, like a general sense of "we're all in this together" community. Most people identified as fellow residents of their neighborhoods, cities or towns, states, country. As members of their religion, or gender, or graduates of this school or that. And ultimately, as fellow members of humanity. Sure, most folks were also pretty tribal about this, referring to their communities or the groups

to which they belonged - or even the teams they rooted for - as "Us",
and everybody in any other group as "Them." And sure, folks who had
less comfort and safety and power tended to be more passionately "Us
versus Them" tribal, jealous of those above them on the social and economic ladders that make up most societies, and eager to have some
group they could look down on, to make themselves feel better.

But for the most part people seemed fairly decent. Respectful of
general norms, accepting of shared moral values about right and wrong.
Focused on themselves and their families first, for sure, but also compassionate toward others, especially those in need. Ready to shovel an
elderly neighbor's walk or donate to their preferred charity. And no
matter how fancy their outward appearance or houses or cars or jewelry or jobs made them seem, at their core most people seemed pretty decent, with common general values - "salt of the earth," as Jesus described
commoners and fishermen in His Sermon on the Mount.

It's not that the people I now interacted with at Harvard weren't
basically the same. They had different interests and styles and back-
grounds and views, and they were caught up in all the unique demands
and pressures of their own lives. But they too were basically decent un-
derneath. It's just that this new community was so narrow compared
to the diverse world I had traveled in for more than 20 years, the one
that taught me to look past the occasional examples of people who were
genuinely despicable and recognize that those examples were the exception, not the norm.

I loved my new environment, but I missed the old one. The big
wide-open world in which I got to meet so many interesting, different
people, in radically different circumstances, all the time. Good people.
Decent people. People who lived by the basic rules, who cared about
their families and friends and communities, who wanted the same basic
things we all do, who laughed and love and joked and cried just like me
and everybody else. People who made me feel like, despite all our dif-

ferences, each of us has a lot in common with all the other passengers in the boat carrying us all, together, down the shared river of our lives.

People like my friend Paula Moore, someone with all those basic, decent values and perceptive human insight, but who also has some special wonderful characteristics, and a unique story, that make her unique.

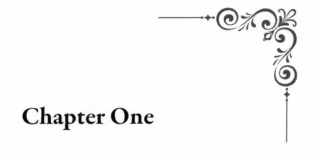

Chapter One

My goodness, the hype on that Saint Patrick's Day in 1997... It was obsessive. The Massachusetts Lottery jackpot had grown to over forty-two million dollars, and people were lining up in droves to get their tickets. The local news stations were leading with the story, dedicating the first several minutes of their broadcasts to interviewing the hopefuls who were standing in line and sharing their dreams. It was all anyone could talk about.

It was a much-needed respite from current events: O.J. Simpson had just been slapped with a massive judgment in the civil trial against him, after which Fred Goldman said he would accept a signed confession to the murder of his son in lieu of payment. The Roslin Institute had recently cloned Dolly the Sheep; but a few days later, President Clinton banned federal funding for that type of research, and people were quite divided on the entire issue.

And something called "The World-Wide Web" was catching on in a big way.

It all got a lot of play in the media, and sparked countless, sometimes contentious discussions among the public, myself included. So this chance at winning the money that would fund a dream life was a welcome diversion from reality.

Although I'd rarely played the Lottery, I found myself caught up in it: the ability to purchase, for a few dollars, the right to spend a couple of days fantasizing. I would pay off debts, of course, then move to New Hampshire. I'd buy houses for my kids, and new cars for everyone in my family. But the priority would be helping my granddaughter Izzy, who was born with cancer. She and my daughter lived next door to me, so I had a front-row seat to their daily struggles. The costs of the treatments, and the travel to and from Boston, was breaking all of us. That was actually the deciding factor for me to head up to the Mobil and buy a ticket.

The store was on the Mass-New Hampshire line, so it was jammed. The long wait allowed ample time to chat with the other daydreamers who waited with me. We were complete strangers, but we shared our lives and exchanged our dream lists. Although I was struck by the shallowness of a few of the comments, there were other stories that left me with a lump in my throat. I mean, of course none of us would win, but the camaraderie among the people in line that day is a memory I carry with me.

When it was my turn to purchase my tickets, I handed the clerk one of those forms where you pick three sets of numbers. I'd used birthdays, anniversaries, and special event dates to pick them.

As I handed him a five-dollar bill, he asked, "Do you want change back, or would you like a couple of Quick-Picks?"

"What's a 'Quick-Pick'?"

He grinned. "We - the machine, actually - will pick the numbers for you."

I thought it over for a moment; then, remembering the crowd of people waiting behind me, I said, "Sure. Why not. Give me two of them."

I tucked my tickets into my purse and headed for home, allowing myself a few more minutes to indulge in some extra daydreaming before real life returned, and then I got lost in trying to figure out what I should make the family for dinner.

I pretty much forgot about the tickets for several days. I would catch an occasional snippet of news on the TV or the radio about people who claimed they'd won, and that the winning ticket had been sold at the Mobil down the street from me. I would glance at the tickets I bought, perched on the shelf that was above my kitchen sink, and admonished the cat to stop playing with them.

A few days later, the media was absolutely exploding about the mystery man who still hadn't claimed his prize. At my candlepin bowling league that week, my teammate Julie asked me, out of nowhere, "Paula, did *you* win that lottery?"

I stared at her, surprised. "What? No. They're saying some guy won it."

"Yeah, he hasn't come forward, so we don't know that. I think *you* won it," she insisted, and I couldn't tell if she was teasing or not. She seemed quite serious.

I was a little distracted after that. I wanted to go home and check those tickets.

I bought a newspaper on the way back to my house and read the numbers: 3,4,6,17,25,45. Bonus: 37.

Those numbers didn't mean anything to me - they didn't match the special dates I'd used. So I brought the paper inside with me and continued reading it while I made supper. At some point, it occurred to me that I had also bought two of those Quick-Picks. I shooed the cat away from the windowsill and picked the tickets up.

One of them contained the winning numbers.

I checked, rechecked, then checked them one more time. I didn't have the Bonus 37, but I had the other six. I think I forgot to breathe for a few seconds, because I felt lightheaded. I quickly sat at the kitchen table and focused on relaxing. I knew I had to have won something substantial, with matching six of the numbers - I figured maybe as much as $50,000. That would be enough to help my daughter and pay off some debts. Maybe after that, we could even have enough left over to move to New Hampshire. To me, moving north was the ultimate in moving up.

I looked around my kitchen, thinking about my beautiful grand-daughter. My children. The bills that had piled up, and the creditors who had been calling more and more frequently in recent days.

Then I looked up to the heavens and smiled. The relief that washed over me became a feeling of absolute joy.

But I had no idea what to do next.

Chapter Two

I decided that calling the Mobil station would be a good place to start. I explained to the pleasant young man who answered the phone that I had the first six numbers, but not the bonus.

He was dead silent for a moment, then he stammered, "Well... You should... Okay, just sign the back and come to the store."

For some reason, I was hesitant to go by myself. I think maybe I wanted someone to be with me to help me hang on to the fact that this was really happening. I called my daughter and told her the news, then asked her to please come with me to the Mobil.

She seemed a little stunned at first. She even asked me to make sure I had the numbers, to check the ticket one more time - which I did, and then I waited for her to settle my granddaughter in with a sitter before we made the two-mile drive to the store.

"I can't *believe* it," she said repeatedly. "And you're really, really sure?"

Every time, I answered with a simple, nervous, "Yup."

When we got to the Mobil, I asked for the owner. I thought I'd get the money right away, or at least in relatively short order. I didn't know anything about how the Lottery worked. Actually, having lived my life as a blue-collar worker whose existence revolved around my family and their needs, I was naïve about a great many things. I had my husband and the kids, my grandchild, my friends, my workaday job, and my bowling league. In spite of our troubles, my life was a comforting and

very familiar cocoon. I had no idea that it was all about to do a dizzying
one-eighty.

The store owner appeared and I held the ticket out for him to see.

"Did you sign it?" he asked.

I nodded as he took it from my hand, then ran it through the machine.

"Well," he said quietly, "you won the jackpot."

I remember my mouth dropping open. "The jackpot? How much
was the jackpot?"

He smiled broadly and covered my hand with his. "Forty-two million dollars."

I stared at him for what had to be several seconds, then I turned to
look at my daughter. She was a little pale, her eyes wide with shock.

"Oh my gosh," I whispered. "Oh my gosh, I can donate to Saint
Monica's now."

"Huh?" she gasped, her hand on her stomach. "You can *what*?"

"You know - they're building that new church," I explained, and
everyone started laughing.

"Go for it," the owner chuckled. "You can buy them the entire
thing, if you want. Lady, you're wicked rich!"

Wicked rich.

My conscious mind rejected it for a minute, while the man at the
counter gave me the details of what I needed to do next.

"You have to take the ticket to Braintree," he was explaining. "Turn
it in there."

I nodded again, then realized I was clinging to my daughter's hand
like a lifeline.

He glanced at the clock. "Dang. It's almost five o'clock," he sighed.
"You'll have to guard this ticket with your life and take it in tomorrow."

He handed it back to me while I nodded yet again. That was all I
could do - nod my head and try to keep my legs under me.

"I'll give them a call for you," he offered, picking up the phone.

I stood staring dumbly at the gum rack while he spoke to the Lottery Bureau. At some point, he turned to me and asked, "Can you get there tomorrow?

Another nod.

He told me that the Lottery Bureau rep wanted to talk to me, and I took the phone from him, grunting a few answers to the wonderfully calm person on the other end.

"This will be public information," he said, "so the media will be there."

"Okay."

Media?

"We'll be sending a limo to bring you here."

"Okay."

Limo?

"Now technically, this isn't a done deal until you bring your ticket in and we verify it. So please, don't let it out of your sight."

"Okay."

No problem there, my friend.

He congratulated me and reminded me to be careful with the ticket before we hung up.

To be honest, I don't remember the ride home, or what - if anything - I said to my daughter. But I remember calling my husband as soon as I got home. He was at his job at an auto parts store.

"Bill..." I hadn't said it out loud yet, and I quickly sat down at the kitchen table. "That forty-two million dollar lottery... I bought the winning ticket."

"Come again?"

I told him what had happened over the past hour. I thought he might scoff, maybe accuse me of playing a joke on him, but he didn't. He was just speechless.

So was my brother, when I called him a few minutes later. Within a couple of hours, we were all in my kitchen being speechless together. It was the quietest my normally raucous family ever was. We were lost in our own thoughts, stunned by the sudden release of so many struggles - problems which, to that point, had harassed us with no end in sight.

I mentioned to Bill that a limo was going to pick us up in the morning, and he needed to wear his Sunday best because the media was going to be there.

He gave me a look of total confusion. I'm sure it mirrored my own.

It was starting to sink in to my conscious mind that this wicked-rich stuff was a wicked big deal.

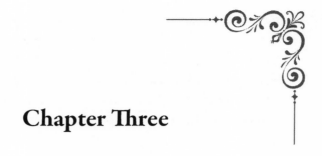

Chapter Three

I stayed awake most of that night, staring at the ticket that was perched on my jewelry box and wishing my mom was still with me. She had passed away four months earlier. I smiled as I imagined her saying, "If the house catches fire, grab that first."

It doesn't matter how old you are. You need your mother. I wanted her to talk with me, to tell me how I was going to handle the new life that was looming just a few hours away. I fretted about what would happen to my family, to myself, and to the rickety but familiar cocoon I'd known for so much of my life and had actually found comfort in.

I spent a good amount of the night reflecting on why *us*. Why *me*. I mean, there had to be so many others who struggled far more than we did, so why were we given this incredible gift?

Obviously, we would want to share the wealth with others. I knew I would have to prioritize the list of those in need - and for some reason, the idea of prioritizing people who needed help struck me as being completely offensive.

Around seven o'clock a.m., I showered and got ready for the day. I thought I should feel nervous, but I didn't. I felt kind of numb, which was probably a good thing. I'd never had to face the media before.

But all that changed around ten o'clock, when the limo arrived. It was a ten-passenger car, and we filled it pretty well: my husband, daughter, and granddaughter came, as did my mother-in-law and my son. As we got closer to Boston, I started feeling giddy and a bit apprehensive. I had no clue about what was going to happen there. I thought

I'd go into some office and hand them the winning ticket, then they would run it through a machine, and I'd leave with a check for forty-two million dollars.

The Lottery reps met us at the limo with their hands extended, offering us their congratulations and a flurry of good wishes. We were escorted into a secluded room where they explained the rules of winning: I had to meet with the media, answer questions, let them take photos, and then I needed to make myself available for a few interviews. Keep in mind that they were asking this of someone whose social anxiety bordered on phobic, and you'll get an idea of how panicked I was becoming.

When we signed the paperwork, I learned that the winnings would be allocated over twenty annual installments. In many ways, that was a huge relief. It seemed more manageable that way. Then we were led to the Media Room and to the dais, where the Lottery Commissioner joined us. I'm glad there is a video available of that press conference, because it seemed to go by in a blur.

I do recall one question in particular, though. A reporter asked, "So, Ms. Moore - you've just won over forty million dollars. What are you going to do first?"

In those days, the expected answer would have been, "I'm going to Disneyland!"

But I tend to be bluntly honest, so I answered truthfully:

"I'm moving to New Hampshire."

That probably wasn't the most tactful response from someone who had just won the Massachusetts Lottery.

The radio interviews were a little less intimidating. It felt more like a conversation and less like being on display. One memorable moment - one that stayed with me - was with a talk show host who, to the point of rudeness, demanded that I admit to his contention that winning the lottery would definitely change me.

"You'll be hiring a driver, traveling the world, eating caviar and living the life of the rich and famous," he insisted, chipping away at my comments about my resolve to stay true to myself.

"You're wrong," I said. I informed him that I would be driving myself around, pumping my own gas, and taking care of my own life.

But he hit a nerve. Deep down, I had been worried about that, as well as the potential for my family to change in negative ways. That was when I decided to alter my priority list - and Priority One would be setting an example for my loved ones: We would stay the same people we always were. The only thing changing here was our bank balance.

Another moment, a rather awkward one, happened when a reporter asked me to tell him about the first check I was going to write.

I said, "The first check is going to go to my church, Saint Monica's, for their renovations."

Another reporter had arrived just after the question, so he heard only my response; as a result, the story he filed stated that I was donating the entire first check to my church. Within a day or so, my pastor called me to tell me that his phone was ringing off the hook with people congratulating him on the windfall.

He invited me over for tea, and we had a lovely talk. At the end, he thanked me for being his "catalyst," because donations for the new church they wanted to build had increased substantially ever since the story came out.

One other reporter, David Ropeik from WCVB's *Chronicle*, became an unexpected friend. Initially, he had contacted me and asked about shadowing me for a year, with his perspective being one of how much I would change in that time. I thought him to be rather smug about it, almost like he was daring me to do it.

I'm a sucker for a dare, so I took him up on it. As that first year went by, he became a very important factor in keeping me grounded. His presence in my life challenged me, and served as a reminder of my commitment to remaining the person I wanted to be. In the end, he showed himself to be an honest, principled, highly insightful young man and a true blessing in my life.

When the parade of interviews concluded, we began to look more closely at our situation. Everyone had advice to offer, and some of it was very useful - especially when it came to our jobs. We heard about a former winner who quit his job, thereby losing his health insurance. Unfortunately, he suffered a heart attack shortly thereafter, and most of his winnings went to medical bills.

Although my husband did decide to stop working, I kept my job and my insurance. As the future unfolded, I was very grateful for that.

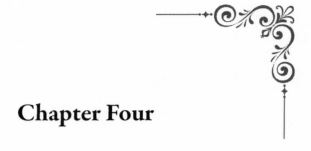

Chapter Four

After the media crush, it was a massive relief to be out of the limelight and finally able to turn my attention to my family's needs. After paying off our debts and consulting with attorneys, we began the process of creating our new life by shopping for new houses for everyone in our family.

My daughter was easy to please. She found an adorable little home on the end of a cul-de-sac in Methuen, and was very glad to be leaving behind the house she'd been living in. She always called it her "haunted house," because a few people had passed away inside it and she was never quite comfortable there.

My son was equally easygoing in choosing his home. Like me, he wanted to live in New Hampshire, so he picked a duplex in Londonderry. It was the perfect size for him, in a lovely neighborhood, and it bordered the woods. He was thrilled with it.

Then it was my turn to find a new home. Having been advised that I should look for higher end homes, which would give me more favorable tax deductions, I decided to give these more opulent houses a look. In the years to come, I would find out that the person who gave me the advice was wrong, but it seemed like a good idea at the time.

I contacted a realtor, giving her an initial budget of $300,000, which I thought was quite a lot of money. Surely, no one needed a property that was more expensive than that - I certainly didn't. But when I mentioned it to my attorney, he insisted that I needed to go much higher.

I reluctantly contacted the realtor again and told her to widen the search. She and my attorney thought I should have a residence in Massachusetts, advising me that the more expensive the house, the better. So we started in Andover with houses that were over a half-million dollars. They were lovely, of course, but I felt like a fish out of water in those neighborhoods. I'd spent the first forty-six years of my life at the same address in Methuen. Until recently, I had been a blue-collar worker, with a twice-mortgaged house and a family that scrapped to get by. I felt that I had nothing in common with the folks in those neighborhoods, and I was terribly uncomfortable.

But I did go to view the homes. One of them was especially interesting: it had been owned by a former professional baseball player, and it was rumored to have a bowling alley in the lower level. It didn't, so I passed on it; however, I had a great couple of days before the viewing, imagining how I would invite my league over for bowling at my house.

The next house was in Methuen. It was simply astounding. It had an year-round enclosed swimming pool, which apparently was the main selling point because it had almost no yard. It also had a price tag that pushed a half-million dollars. I simply couldn't see myself living there - it was just too much of everything. I pictured myself spending most of my time at home, cleaning and maintaining what should be my refuge, so I passed on that one, as well. I was starting to think that perhaps I should just buy a home I liked instead of a house that was a savvy investment, but I continued to follow the advice of others.

Then my husband happened to notice a property on the cover of a New Hampshire real estate magazine. The picture showed a long driveway that led to a stately waterfront home, fronted by an expansive and beautifully manicured front lawn. My heart leaped - this was the first house that truly appealed to me.

We called our realtor right away, and we were terribly disappointed to find out that the house had just been pulled from the market.

"But let me make a few calls," she said.

She managed to get us a showing, and even though the asking price was over $500,000, we had barely pulled into the driveway when I turned to my husband and said, "I don't care what it looks like inside. I'm absolutely crazy about this house."

The interior was even more stunning than I'd imagined. It was quite large, with high ceilings, a sunken formal living room, and a massive lower level that had a built-in bar. I fell head-over-heels in love with it. I could see myself living there. Sure, it was a little too much square footage for my tastes: four bedrooms and four bathrooms seemed excessive. After all, I came from a place where trying to gain access to our one bathroom was like trying to book a vacation on Martha's Vineyard in July; however, the property had several decks that looked out over the pond, and that put it over the top for me.

We put an offer in immediately, which the owners accepted, and then made our move to New Hampshire in May of 1997. Finally, both my lawyer and I were happy.

I loved living in New Hampshire. I still do. There's a quiet simplicity to life in this beautiful state: an independent, rugged, yet peaceful atmosphere that encourages people to work hard, play hard, and dream big. To live free.

Throughout the course of the next two years, we acquired a summer cottage on the beach and a getaway house in Las Vegas. We also helped my brother with a property in Methuen, and my mother-in-law with her purchase of a house right down the street from us - one that she was thrilled with until the day she actually moved into it. We eventually relocated her to a lovely condominium in Salem, New Hampshire, and she settled right in.

At the same time, we decided to upgrade my daughter's home. We swapped out her Cape Cod-style house for something upscale in Bedford, New Hampshire. Then we upgraded our son's duplex into a lovely, larger single-family home.

With that, the househunting was finally done, as was the seemingly endless initial to-do list - which I think, looking back, was quite beneficial to my adjustment period. I didn't have a lot of time to think.

I was excited, relieved, and more than a little apprehensive. Up to that point, my life had been relatively predictable, with only a few distractions that mixed with the occasional serious issue. I thought often of the comments of those who insisted that I would change, and I worried about it. More than that, I worried about my family - about holding everything and everyone together. I had my doubts as to whether or not I could do that.

But ready or not, it was time to settle into my new life and leave the old one behind.

Perhaps it's more accurate to say that it was time to leave my old life*style* behind, because there were - and are - parts of myself that I'll never surrender.

Chapter Five

I was born in 1950 into a family that was so completely Massachusetts blue-collar, it was almost a caricature of the industrious, lower middle-class people whose life is a daily scuffle for survival.

We were poor, really, but I never knew it. My mother, a homemaker who managed to elevate her calling to an art form, was the center of our home. She could stretch a dollar like a rubber band, so my big brother and I wanted for nothing that a child needs. None of the truly important things, anyway, like food, clothing, education, and her abundant love and attention. We had dinner together every evening; every Sunday, we gathered for a traditional meal, usually a roast that would become the main ingredient of the following week's dinners. I remember running home from school, looking forward to her Shepherd's Pie, meatloaf, or thick beef stew over mashed potatoes - what we now call the "comfort foods" that are now branded as being unhealthy. Even deadly.

You know, I long for the simplicity and innocence of those times. I think we all had far less stress back in the days before we were inundated with dire warnings about all of the things that can kill us. I've often wondered why the well-educated among us spend so much time wringing their hands because we all won't live to age ninety-five, and if the constant fretting over the length of life - versus the *quality* of it - has cost us more than we realize. If nothing else, putting life under a microscope serves only to shroud our ability to enjoy it.

As a little girl, securely nested in a life that made sense to me, I did enjoy it. I was a Daddy's Girl, tagging along with my father whenever I could. He worked for the Methuen Department of Public Works, but picked up side projects like plowing or home improvements, and he'd take me along with him on those jobs. I learned a lot of life lessons from those adventures with my dad, not the least of which was the value of hard work and the incomparable feeling of satisfaction that comes from a difficult job that is done well.

But my father was also a drunk, a fact that I allowed to sink in slowly as I got older. He was a functioning alcoholic for many years, but eventually it caught up with him and it cost him his job.

It cost the rest of us a whole lot more.

Holidays were the worst. As far back as I can remember, I longed for the love and serenity that was depicted on Christmas cards and Norman Rockwell holiday prints: happy families around beautiful Thanksgiving tables, and glittery winter scenes that adorned the joyful greetings that came in the mail. Of course, we wore the façade of holiday cheer wherever we needed to; however, the years became decades, which then became a legacy - one of planning and preparing for an annual disillusionment, through which I quietly withdrew inside myself. My father would get falling-down drunk, the arguing and the ugliness would escalate, and then it would erupt.

So I would retreat into my coping mechanism of working toward a better future. I wanted to build a happy life, one I would control, fully insulated from the sickness that stole my family from me.

Eventually, I grew to despise the holidays. My celebrations were reserved for the day after, when I could return to a life that held no expectations and therefore, no disappointments.

As anyone in close proximity to an alcoholic can attest to, insecurity and crises, even disasters become commonplace. Eventually, the chaos becomes a state of normalcy. And since you have no power to affect the situation, you adapt.

In my case, I developed a stone-wall sense of pragmatism. When your life is lived in a grim anticipation of the roof caving in, you tend to spend your time either staring at the roof, or planning the future while you pretend that the roof isn't there. Either way, the idea of "happily ever after" becomes a trigger for cynicism, and that's what I became: cynical. My brother did as well. Not entirely, but enough that it divided us.

As children, my brother and I were generally close, but we began to drift apart through a painful period of time that seemed to evolve as our dad declined. We were growing up, and of course our lives were taking separate courses; however, I think my brother and I fell into that strange dynamic that perhaps adult children of alcoholics know all too well. We had been raised in a house that was infected by alcoholism, and addiction seems to create an atmosphere of humiliation - a self-conscious discomfort that makes it hard to connect with others. We've found our way back to each other in recent years, but I grieve for the years we lost.

It was hard to keep my bearings, but Mom... She was my guiding light. As I got older, she became my best friend. Sure, I had my youthful episodes of driving her crazy, especially when it came to the boys I dated. I was almost always drawn to the bad boy type. In the rare instance that Mom approved of one of my boyfriends, I dumped him. If she disapproved, my rebellious teenage mind processed that as a rousing thumbs-up.

My behavior had to be especially difficult for her, since Mom had medical issues that were quite pronounced when I was young. She would let me spend summers with my favorite cousin, nine years my senior, so I could have a reprieve from the problems in our house and just enjoy myself. Those were good times for me, although I doubt that Mom would have approved of my adventures with my cousin. Remember, this was the 1960's, during the days of Haight-Ashbury and the Hippies, Students for a Democratic Society and Flower Power. But my cousin, very much like a big sister to me, retained few of those high-minded ideals. She simply taught me how to smoke, shave my legs, and other things that I thought heralded my entry into the Sixties Counterculture. I did no drugs or anything like that, but every summer, we definitely ran counter to the world that was my mother's culture.

Still, Mom was the constant in my life, the one with all the answers. The one who never failed to come running when I called out for her.

Education was important to her, but equally important was knowledge. Wisdom. Looking back, I now understand how devoted she was to developing not only my mind, but also my soul - to imparting upon me the intangible but essential life skills of common sense and character.

In spite of her efforts, though, I was just an average student. It wasn't that I didn't work hard enough; I simply wasn't the scholarly type at that point in my life. There was this big, exciting world out there, with so much to see and do, and I wanted to be out there in it.

My years in middle school accommodated that desire, because we had double sessions that allowed me to go to school in the morning and work in the afternoon. I got a job at what is now Holy Family Hospital, making ten dollars a week working in the Payroll Department. I found that my father was right: there's nothing like accepting your paycheck at the end of a long week. The experience at Holy Family set me on a course in life of always working, and always doing my absolute best on the job.

My favorite person there was Sister Alberta, a nun who worked at the hospital. I think she saw in me a business acumen worth developing, so she had me doing Accounts Payable and Receivable as well as Payroll, which I learned on the monstrous machines they used in the early 1960's. She certainly didn't have much money, but she was the one who reached into her pocket and paid me my ten dollars every week. Eventually, she had me sitting by the elevators handing out paychecks to the staff - even the doctors, which was a source of pride for me since I was only thirteen. I never forgot the confidence she had in me.

Between my mom and Sister Alberta - and in spite of my middling grades - I developed a passion for working in general and business in particular. I took business classes in high school, and worked nights and weekends at either the hospital or in the kitchen of a nursing home. With my schedule, I never had the time to join any clubs or groups, which was fine with me because I was quite shy. I had very few friends, I never went to any of the parties or dances that the other kids went to - I never even went to any of the concerts that were becoming more and more popular in those days. In the sixties, basic morality was being burned alongside flags, bras, and draft cards, and drugs were more and more widely used. I didn't want any part of it. I think that was the era when good kids were shunned into the underground, and in our absence, the culture started to implode.

So after graduation, I took my square and decidedly un-groovy self to a hairdressing school, and shortly after that, I got a job at the IRS. I didn't need a college degree to work there, which was a good thing, since I had no money for a university degree.

During those years, I met a neighborhood guy who was friends with a cousin of mine. His name was Bill. I thought Bill was a bit of a bad boy, in stark contrast to my good Catholic girl image, but he was absolutely adorable. Full lips, dark hair, real attitude - and he wouldn't give me the time of day.

We used to have a huge annual gathering at the beach with all of the extended families there. At the get-together right after I graduated, my cousin invited Bill to join us. I had invited a friend to stay over with me at the beach, and after sharing with her my desire to meet Bill, we decided that all I needed was a shot of courage. Several shots, actually, from a bottle of Boone's Farm Apple Wine that we discovered in one of the cottages that were rented for the family.

Keep in mind that I never drank alcohol. *Ever.*

I was high as a kite within an hour, at which point I went to find Bill. I talked to him for a while, then kissed him right on those bad-boy lips... And then I puked all over the place.

I was twenty-three when we got married. My mom wasn't happy with my choice at first, but she adjusted to it. Bill and I managed to set up a decent, simple life, with both of us working. I was still at the IRS, and Bill went to work for an auto parts store for a while, until his life-long desire to own his own business took him over. He and a couple of buddies decided to open a siding business, one that was funded almost entirely by us and died rather quickly, I believe mostly from neglect.

I supported his project as best I could, even though we were working opposite schedules - I worked nights and he worked days - but by the time I got to the point of total frustration, the business was gone. Bill returned to his former job at the auto parts store.

We had settled in the house I grew up in, a duplex, with Mom and Dad living on one side and us in the other, paying them twenty dollars a week in rent. It was a nondescript little place that was very much the standard house for a blue-collar Methuen family: old, somewhat run down, and needing repairs that always got pushed aside for our more pressing necessities. We managed to get by, but it wasn't easy.

In 1975, I gave birth to my son; my daughter, whom I call my "Bicentennial Baby," was born the following year. They were sweet, loving, intelligent children, and I fully enjoyed my years as a young mother.

But I sometimes felt like I was failing my children. I often longed for them to have a nicer home to bring their friends to, which was something they seldom did. I really couldn't blame them. I wished that we lived in a better neighborhood, had more money, and I longed for a warmer, more welcoming home for them. Theirs was a stressful, sometimes chaotic upbringing that reminded me of my own in some ways, because shades of addiction seemed to move in, sitting smugly in the middle of our house. Again.

It filtered through slowly, like these things tend to do, but eventually I suspected that I had married and had children with a man who was very much like my father. It certainly seemed that way to me. He smoked, and drank, and holidays were often an exercise in damage control; but overall, it seemed peaceful in our house when compared to the chaos between my own parents, because Bill and I still worked opposite schedules. We didn't spend a lot of time together. I think that's the reason it took so long for me to see the reality of the problems in our marriage - which also included financial problems that I was not aware of. Bill was the one who handled the finances in the early years of our marriage, so I didn't discover the enormous amount of debt we were in until the creditors started calling.

I was shocked to discover that we were thousands of dollars in debt. Actually, I was horrified. When the dust settled, the pragmatic part of me emerged and went into high gear, and I took over full control of the family finances. I created a plan and attacked the debts in the most orderly manner I could, paying the minimum on the larger bills and whittling away at the smaller ones.

I knew it would be a years-long struggle. As organized as I was about it, the incredible, unnecessary waste of our already emaciated budget wore me down into despair at times. I felt like I was alone, doing penance for another's failings, and living inside the emotional shelter-in-place existence that follows a deep betrayal.

At the time, I had no idea it was the beginning of the end of my marriage.

Chapter Six

There were good times. Of course there were. I have children who make me indescribably proud, and grandchildren who are the world to me. I've never had many close friends, but I wouldn't trade the special people who welcome me into their lives for anything. I've had a wonderful and satisfying career that has been very meaningful to me, and I was blessed with the ability to do some good in the world.

Yet as I look back, it seems to me that my life to age forty-seven prepared me to better appreciate all that I have, probably to a far greater extent than I otherwise would have. It was like all the bad things were frontloaded for me, and those experiences made me angry at the way evil works its way into good people: quietly, unobtrusively, pretending to be just a bad habit or a lapse in judgment until the day it hits you like a two-by-four to the head.

As the years went by, my father was drinking more and more, getting to the point of choking and sometimes becoming cyanotic. I would check on him as often as possible, raising his arms over his head so he could breathe. Eventually, and I hate to admit this, it became more of a chore than anything else. He was so far inside his addiction, it was like the booze took over his body, and Dad - the man he might have been, I mean - simply ceased to exist.

On July 4, 1976, he drank even more than usual and was combative all night. I lived next door to Mom and Dad in the duplex, so I could hear what was going on.

On July fifth, I heard him in their bathroom washing up. I thought about checking on him, but I didn't have the time at that moment. Then when it got quiet over there, I assumed he was sleeping it off.

As I opened my front door to go run a few quick errands, I was greeted by my dog, galloping toward me and shrieking more than barking. It was a noise she'd never made before, and it was absolutely chilling. I followed her over to the other side of the house, into the living room where it appeared that my father was asleep on the sofa.

I yelled at the dog to stop barking, afraid that she would awaken him. Then I noticed he was blue.

"Dad?"

He was motionless. I said it again.

"*Dad.*"

I tried once more, this time trying to yell his name, but I couldn't get any breath behind it.

The few steps it took to get to the sofa felt like I was walking in quicksand. I touched his face and he was ice cold.

"Oh, Dad," I whispered. "Oh no."

I called 911 and told them I thought my father might be dead, but I knew that he was.

Waiting for the paramedics to arrive, I found myself reflecting on his life, willing myself to remember only the good things about him. I wanted his life to mean something - not only to me, but to the world, because no one is born into this world without leaving their unique, inimitable mark on it. I thought he could have been so much more if his time hadn't run out. He was only fifty-six years old.

I followed the ambulance to the hospital, the same one where my mother worked, trying to figure out how I would break the news to her. I hoped I would find her quickly, before anyone else had the opportunity to tell her. I wanted her to hear it from me.

When I arrived, she was standing right there in the corridor. I had the impression that she was waiting for me. Her expression was calm and a little sorrowful, like she was worried about *me*. I was quite sure that there hadn't yet been time for anyone to tell her what had happened, but I asked her if they had.

She touched my cheek and answered, "No. But he's gone, isn't he?"

"Yeah, Mom. He is."

She nodded slowly. "I just had a feeling. Are you okay?"

I wasn't sure how to answer, because the truth made me feel like maybe I was a bad daughter. I *was* okay. I'd spent most of my life preparing myself for that day, and I felt like the way he died had been the foregone conclusion to his life for so long, I had completed my grieving while he was still alive.

"I'm fine, Mom."

She nodded again, like she already knew that, as well.

Witnessing her composure, I realized something that had never occurred to me before that moment: Mom, too, had prepared herself for that day. She had already done her grieving, just as I had; more than that, through the years of living with an alcoholic, she had become accustomed to being alone. She was ready for this. As I thought about our family, four people who were isolated within in the grip of an addict and his chaotic life - and who were divided and conquered by it - I suddenly discovered that I had yet another reason to grieve.

The atmosphere in our house was somber after the funeral, with all of us staying close to each other and talking very little; but eventually, we returned to our day-to-day lives. It was then that I noticed that my mother was different somehow. She seemed to be opening up. Perhaps it's better said that she was *re*opening, like her heart, soul, and mind had become unburdened. She even seemed happy at times. She had peace.

As for me... Perhaps because of the chaos that is so much a part of growing up in an addicted home, which is a climate and a lifestyle that normalizes trauma, I absorbed the reality of Dad's death with the same practicality I applied to my life as a whole. At least, I believed I did.

Now that I can revisit it from the vantage point of time gone by, I think my grief eventually became anger. Not a fruitless, belligerent resentment that colored my ability to learn and grow and love; actually, I developed a deep, quiet outrage at the influences that destroy souls - the forces that ferret out our weaknesses, plant seeds of dissatisfaction, and then water those seeds with self-deception. As you've probably already surmised, I especially despise addiction. It's everywhere, and it's destroying lives.

As a culture, and especially here in New Hampshire, we see it all around us. Moreover, we're so shocked by its devastation that I wonder if we run the risk of fully normalizing drug usage, much like an addict's family unit will fall into normalizing the source of their own trauma.

I used to believe that all of our cultural ills, including addiction, were enabled by ignorance. Now I think the machine that keeps them going is a widespread sense of being overwhelmed. At this point in our history, with an entire world that is informed to maximum capacity by the World Wide Web, few can claim a lack of knowledge about the issues that can steal our humanity. Yet the same social media that informs us has also led us to be both the deceptive and the deceived, allowing us to craft an image that reveals only the enviable aspects of our lives, or displays the attention-seeking behavior that keeps attention-starved people hungry. As a result, too many people disappear inside their addiction to technology, finding comfort there and then becoming enslaved to manipulating the thoughts and opinions of their audience. Others believe that sharing a story, hitting "Like" on a post, or developing a creative hash tag means they've done their part to affect a "change" - one that they too often can't describe, define, or even understand. And the chaos rolls merrily on.

We're overloaded with incessant input, with little time to process before the next crisis starts trending - again, much like the experience of living with an addict. Unmanaged, it's easy to become hopeless. To lose ourselves inside the need to be accepted.

I decided early on in my life, I think around the time I got married, that I would protect my sense of self and my beliefs about right and wrong, and I would guard myself against the loneliness that comes from refusing to follow the crowd. I was never any good at cultivating popularity; as I got older, I realized it was because I wasn't all that interested in doing so. Someplace in my soul, I knew that the biggest mistake we make is in trying to force ourselves to be accepted by the world. That mirage of inclusion is perhaps the most powerful lure into a life of subservient futility.

In other words, I decided that I would always be exactly who I am. Winning the lottery was an unexpected, astonishing, often disheartening challenge to my resolution.

Chapter Seven

After I collected the first installment of my lottery winnings, the first thing I wanted to do - other than deliver a check to Saint Monica's - was to get out of debt.

Actually, I think the main reason Saint Monica's got their donation before I wrote our creditors off was because it was on the way home from the Lottery Bureau. I couldn't wait to be free of the heaviness that had weighed me down for so long, the dread of the headache-inducing balancing act that was paying the monthly bills. I'd spent years weighing need versus want, then dismissing all wants and prioritizing needs, then wrestling with the pros and cons of each need to make sure it was truly an essential. I was looking forward to a life with no financial concerns.

Then a friend who knows about these things gave me a warning. He said, "Paula, you *still* have money problems. Lots of them, maybe even more than you had before. They're just different problems now." He gave me a regretful look and added, "You'll see what I mean."

He was so right. Although the relief of being debt-free was absolutely heavenly, and being able to provide a better life for my family was an unimaginable, impossible dream, I often did battle with myself. I regularly found myself alternating between my desire to indulge in extravagances and my need to stay on top of the family finances.

Of course, I did want us to have the finer things in life, but I was afraid of running through the money too quickly. By the time we had everyone riding in new cars and situated in new homes, over ninety percent of the first year's check was gone. Yes, there was still a high balance in my account, but I learned that the speed with which it could drop was unnerving. So I decided to put my accounting background to good use and create a budget. I took a little flack for that at first, and there were times when I wondered if I was being a total killjoy; however, I'd heard lots of stories about lottery winners who wound up penniless, and I had no intention of becoming another anecdote about bad choices and the things that might have been.

I was also torn by the cards and letters I received from others, many of whom were total strangers, asking for financial help. Some of the stories were heartbreaking. I was particularly moved by the needs of those who were trying to better themselves, especially women who were struggling with the incredible expense of higher education. As much as I wanted to write every one of them a check, I knew that wasn't feasible, so I decided to create an endowment for them at Northern Essex Community College.

I was taking classes there at the time that I won the lottery, working toward twenty-four credits in Accounting in order to save my job at the IRS, and paying for my classes with a credit card. I knew the stress of going into debt for an education that was necessary for a better life. The scholarship that I funded provided assistance for women who were returning to college, and to me, it was one of the most meaningful results of winning the lottery.

One woman in particular has stayed in my thoughts throughout the years. As a thank-you to NECC for accommodating those of us who needed to be recertified as tax professionals every year, I volunteered to do taxes there for students who needed the service.

As I was packing my supplies one evening, getting ready to wrap up the day, a middle-aged woman came rushing in.

"Are you closing up?" she asked breathlessly.

I needed to go pick up my grandchild, but I glanced at my watch and decided there was time to do one more tax return.

"Have a seat," I said. 'What do you need?"

She told me she'd had her taxes done by one of the big-name tax companies, and wound up owing two thousand dollars because she neglected to have taxes withheld from her unemployment benefits.

"I got laid off," she explained, "and I really needed the extra money to get by."

I remember thinking, *Yikes. This is going to be bad.*

"Did you find another job?" I asked.

She nodded. "But I'm barely making ends meet, and they want nearly five hundred dollars before they'll process my returns. I got an email about your service here, and I just had a feeling that you would help."

I engaged her in conversation while we did her returns, asking her about the classes she was taking. She told me she was studying to be a drug counselor, so of course, I felt an instant connection to her for that alone.

Then she said the magic words: "I'm so afraid I won't be able to finish school. It's tough being my age and going back to college. It's so *expensive.*"

I can't describe the rush of gratitude that went through me, and the thrill of knowing I could help. There's no better feeling than that moment when someone shares a pressing need, and you're in the right place at the right time, able fill it for them immediately.

I told her about the endowment for women just like her, then suggested that she apply for it right away - because I would place a few calls to make sure it was awarded to her. She cried, she hugged me, but I suspect she never knew how deeply our brief encounter affected me.

Many of the cards and letters I received after the win were every bit as poignant, and to this day, I still wonder how those people are doing. There were requests for help with paying bills, medical expenses, credit cards, and funding for school projects. There were people asking me to please buy their house before they went into foreclosure. Others asked for money for loved ones or friends. Those were especially difficult to read, especially when the problem they wrote about was an illness. A young mother wrote me about her sadness that she hadn't picked the right numbers, and shared her problems with me to the point where she had me in tears.

We all know about and care for the people who have far more than their fair share of life's problems, but that concern is taken to an entirely different level when they reach out to you knowing that you have the means to help. Then the heartbreaking truth hits you when you realize that you can't help them all. The sorrow can be crushing. I tried at first to read every letter, but I have to admit, it got to be overwhelming. I eventually decided to address their needs by donating to charities and organizations that they could access for assistance. I hope it helped them, and that those who shared their stories with me know how deeply I cared about their struggles.

But there were some messages that made me smile, as well as others that had me laughing aloud. I even got offers from people who wanted to train me in a new career. Sometimes, however, a letter would arrive that scared me. An especially memorable request came from a man who asked me to leave him an envelope in my mailbox with cash in it for the next morning, assuring me he'd stop by to retrieve it before the mailman arrived. I had a few unsettled days after that one.

More than anything else, I treasured the cards and notes from my friends and neighbors. I heard from people whom I hadn't seen in years, and it felt wonderful to know that they remembered me. Although I was uncomfortable that they would congratulate me for winning - I mean, it was a stroke of luck, and not anything I'd done to deserve it - their good wishes were an important, reassuring anchor in my suddenly upside-down life.

I have to confess to frequent feelings of guilt, though. Perhaps it was more of a "why *me*?" kind of thing that I tried to manage through charitable efforts, but I'll always be grateful for the chance I was given to help people. Beyond the joy of being able to give to others, doing so helped to fill some of the voids that were created by becoming suddenly wealthy. As it turned out, there were quite a few, and they ran deep.

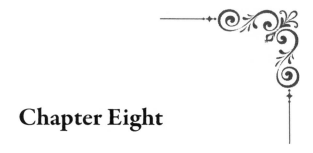

Chapter Eight

We were settled into our new waterfront home in New Hampshire by the summer of that year. It was a joyous time, and not only because of how much I loved the house: it felt wonderful to be debt-free, done with relocating and getting our family members settled in, and completely moved in to our new place. I'd discarded or donated almost all of the contents of the old house in Methuen, keeping only memorabilia like important pictures and keepsakes. Then I had the time of my life with furnishing and decorating my dream home.

It was finally time for us to enjoy ourselves. I couldn't wait to share it with our friends.

But it seemed like many of our old friends had fallen away. They appeared to be uncomfortable just dropping by like they used to, or calling to see if we were busy that night in case we wanted to join them for a movie or a game of cards. I missed them, and I wondered what was wrong.

At some point, it occurred to me that I would probably feel some uncertainty or ambivalence if one of *my* good friends had won the lottery. I remembered all the people who kept telling me I would change, that I would no longer be the same old Paula, and I thought it might be that very notion which was creating the distance between our friends and us. So I decided to have a celebration - a big, happy bash of a house party, just to reconnect and show them that the only thing different about us was our address.

Party Day was in September, and even the capricious New England weather decided to cooperate. It was going to be a picture-perfect afternoon for sunning by the pond and grilling burgers. I planned the menu, bought the beer and the wine, and made sure the house looked warm and welcoming. I was so excited that so many of our friends said they would show up that I spent the morning running around like a little kid, enjoying the preparations and giggling to myself. I couldn't wait to see them all again, catch up on their lives, and let them see that I was the same person they'd know for so many years.

Of course, the fact that Channel Five's *Chronicle* showed up to cover the event put a big dent in my plans for a private display of homespun hospitality. By that time, I'd become somewhat used to being followed by the press, and I was able to maneuver around them and still enjoy the party. My friends, however, weren't accustomed to looking into TV cameras and being asked questions, and I regretted that I didn't anticipate their discomfort. I should have. Although many of them seemed to enjoy the experience, it made others uncomfortable and the distance between us more acute, and my natural tendency to withdraw started to kick in.

The gathering wasn't exactly like I envisioned. It was fun, but also strained at times, and I found myself trying perhaps a little too hard to be my old self - which meant, of course, that I was nothing like my old self. More than that, the piece which aired on *Chronicle* highlighted not only our nouveau affluence, but in doing so, revealed the disconnect between my friends and me. At one point, the camera captured one of our guests commenting on the resentment and jealousy, even hatefulness of some of the old crowd, and I remember cringing when I saw it. It was a devastating moment. We did have some success in reclaiming our old relationships, but I realized that many of them were lost forever.

After that, I threw myself into my job and working toward my college degree, which I was determined to complete. The time I spent on campus was the closest thing to normalcy in my life back then. The people there, especially the kids, treated me like I was just another student. It was a huge comfort, very much the only place of quiet refuge outside of my home.

But my job at the IRS was a different story. The union there wasn't crazy about me or my management style, and they wanted me to quit.

The climate there also seemed to reflect the idea that I was taking a job away from someone who really needed it. It got ugly enough that someone actually went as far as to hang my picture on the wall with the caption, *What do we need to do to get rid of this woman?* When I started receiving direct threats to my safety, I had to be escorted from the building every time I left. Some of the people there had decided for me that I had no right to work. Since I had money now, why should I be working anyway?

Because I wanted to. I needed to. There are reasons that people work that have nothing to do with income, but my refusal to quit seemed to irritate them to no end. They became overtly hostile toward me, delivering cutting comments and sotto voce insults as I walked by, pretending they weren't saying it loudly enough for me to hear. Then they looked at me in wide-eyed innocence if I turned to confront them. Apparently they didn't know me well enough to realize that I don't back down to bullies, I never run from a fight, and I don't abandon my responsibilities.

Yet in spite of my inherent stubbornness, I did have a run of sleepless nights which actually got me to thinking about quitting; moreover, when I thought about the many friends who were now gone from my life, I considered the idea of simply walking away from everyone and everything I'd known to that point. After all, I'd already left my old lifestyle behind - why not abandon my old life?

As I sat on my deck and stared out over the water one morning, encouraging my own resentment to take over my heart and mind, it became clear to me that others had already made that choice for me. And that's when I came to understand how people lose themselves.

It was a spiritual battle, one that was all about whether or not I would surrender. Not necessarily to the people who had turned away from us, or to those who were trying to drive me from my work... But giving in to anger, to the envy that is the natural result of comparing our lives to what we think others have. I was very close to joining them in *their* surrender to the forces which seek only to destroy souls. As much as I'd tried to retain my sense of self, I was wavering.

It made me angry, but in a different way. This amazing gift had been given to us, a blessing through which we could bless others, and it was being sullied by forces that I had no control over. Well, I wasn't about to let it change *me*. I certainly wasn't going to be like *them*.

Spiritual battles can be like a game of Whack-a-Mole, can't they?

Right there, I caught another burgeoning attitude within myself, one that had the potential to fully destroy not only my gratitude, but my ability to forgive others: I was developing a warped, defensive sense of superiority over the people I had loved for so long. In my resolution to not be like them, I was actually judging them. More than that, devoting too much of my mental energy to what I *didn't* want to be would, by definition, impact who I was.

I realized that more than anything else, I needed to forgive them. I needed to honestly understand and keep loving them, no matter what became of our relationships. It was a hard lesson, and it hurt. Truly letting go and wishing them well, knowing that they might never return to my life, taught me the real meaning of forgiveness and why it's essential to our own souls.

I remembered all the people who told me I would change. It seemed that the naysayers were on to something after all: money changes people, which changes everyone around them - including me, if I allowed it. Bitterness almost took me over, and it has more sticky strands than a spider web.

At that moment, I fully understood the concept of being separate. In my entire life, I'd never felt so lonely.

Chapter Nine

The first autumn at the lake house was absolutely exquisite. The fall colors in New Hampshire are a natural wonder that defies description, and the clean, cool air creates deep blue skies that are the perfect backdrop for the foliage.

The entire family was settled in, the kids were doing well, and I was still going in to my job at the IRS while working toward my Accounting degree. I still worked the food counter serving hot dogs at my Thursday night Bingo games, went bowling, and watched football. We weren't completely adjusted to our routine yet, but life was comparatively peaceful.

One of the first things Bill did after the win was to quit his job at the auto parts store; however, after a six-month respite, he was getting bored. He decided he wanted to go back to work, so he talked me into buying a travel agency. It seemed like a good idea, because I knew it was the kind of work he would enjoy and I was glad that he wanted to get active again. I was getting very busy with the Y2K conversion at work, since I was a Team Leader on the project, so I knew I'd be preoccupied with that. I agreed to buy the agency.

He liked it at first, learning new things and handling all the details that go with running a business. As time went by, though, I found out that the agency was financially on the ropes, so I went over there myself to find out what had gone wrong.

It didn't take long to figure out that several of the employees were not doing their jobs. More than that, the waste and inefficiency was ruining the business. I took some classes in travel and hospitality to supplement my business and accounting education, then began working there myself. I wound up firing several workers who were running the place into the ground. A few others quit, but the employees who truly cared about doing their jobs stayed - some for over fifteen years, until I retired.

I initially decided to run the agency in order to save it, then stayed on because of how much I loved the work. It turned out to be one of the happier times of my life. Not only did I get to put my business sense to good use, but it was a breeze to put together the trips I wanted to take and package the events that I wanted to attend. Since most of my clientele was made up of working Baby Boomers, I would create packages that I thought they would enjoy - which was quite easy, as I was a working Baby Boomer myself.

One of my favorite trips was going to New York for the Macy's Parade. It was the warmest Thanksgiving Day on record, the parade went right past our hotel room, and we got to bring our lawn chairs so we could watch it up close. The pageantry of it is so much more exciting when you're right there with it.

The most memorable day trip was spending the Fourth of July on the Charles in Boston. It was a dinner cruise attended by almost sixty clients to watch the fireworks from the private boat I chartered. Neil Diamond was the star performer that year, and we had what amounted to a front-row seat.

But there was one vacation that will always be especially meaningful to me. Truth be told, it was more like paying a debt of gratitude than a vacation.

When I was a teenager, there was a family in our neighborhood whose home was the place where we obnoxious teens were always welcomed. It was a happy, noisy Italian home, and I would usually just sit and enjoy the conversations and the laughter, especially over the holidays. It was something of a refuge for me, a place where I could leave behind the chaos in my own house. As the years went by, these people welcomed my children as if they were their own grandchildren. I never forgot those wonderful, loving neighbors who made me feel like part of their family at a time when I needed it so badly.

After I won the lottery, I asked the patriarch, who was now a widower and almost eighty years old, if he would let me take him to see Italy. It took him a few minutes to recover from the surprise of the invitation, but then he said that all things considered, he would much prefer to see Ireland. Since I'm half Irish, and I won the lottery on St. Patrick's Day, it seemed meant to be. We hosted both him and his daughter.

It was my first time seeing Ireland, and it was even more beautiful than I'd imagined. He said that the same was true for him. That trip is a memory that I will always keep close to my heart.

Bill and I took the time to indulge in a few other extravagances during that first year, like trips to Hollywood and the Caribbean. Our vacation in Las Vegas was the most fun I'd ever had.

We took our best friends with us as an anniversary gift to them. Danielle was a friend since high school; her husband, Sean, was an old friend of Bill's, so it was a good mix. We stayed at The Mirage, saw the sights, and enjoyed a little of the gambling.

I found my all-time favorite game, Bingo, at The Monte Carlo. *Chronicle* had followed us out there, since it was still part of the first year and they were recording my experiences, and the cameras caught me whispering to Danielle about the next number I needed in order to win the game. Sure enough, the one I needed came up at exactly that moment and I yelled, "Bingo!"

A short while later, I was at the slot machines. I won the jackpot - which in those days came out as a noisy deluge of coins - and they got that on film, as well. One of the other players made the comment that I couldn't lose for winning, and I admit, I was a little embarrassed by it. But we had a lot of fun and countless laughs, the best one being at the Blackjack table where someone mistook my husband for the singer Meatloaf.

Although WCVB was there with us, they managed to be discreet and didn't impact the trip much at all. Actually, of all the media that followed us around, the people from that station were the most respectful. They were sensitive, even kind to me. They had real journalistic integrity, and I admired and very much appreciated what a class act they were. I never felt mocked or exploited by them. Not to say that other outlets were less than professional, not at all; however, Channel Five seemed to go out of their way to be accommodating and fair-minded.

I can't say the same about many other news sources, though. Sometimes I had the feeling there was some kind of a fixation on me, like an almost obsessive component to the media coverage of the win and my life afterwards. I truly didn't understand it, because I never considered myself to be all that interesting; however, there was nothing I could do to stop it, so I learned to adapt.

There were articles about me that were purely informational, which of course I had no issues with. I knew that I, too, would have been curious. There were some that were simply irritating, like the national tabloid that called me "Granny" and wrote an entire article around the fact that I was still working. A local paper ran a story with a big headline that read, "Lottery Winner Dares to Be Boring," then went on to share the fact that I'd bought twelve pairs of tube socks at a local Wal-Mart with my winnings.

I was honestly bewildered by the fact that it was important enough to make the news. I *needed* tube socks.

Another article reported that I won $150 at Bingo. I eventually found out that not many people took notice of the fact that I donated it right back.

Many of the features that were done about me seemed to revolve around my desire to continue working, and for the life of me, I still can't comprehend why *that* would be a story of any interest to anyone.

Of all the coverage and the comments to or about me, the ones which expressed complete incredulity that I would remain a hard working, frugal woman were the most annoying.

Still other news articles were embarrassing. My donation to St. Monica's was covered repeatedly, and since I believe that such things should be as private as possible, I regretted sharing my donation plans at the press conference on the day I got the first check. Another source of embarrassment was the media coverage of the day I got the Outstanding Alumna Award from Northern Essex Community College. That piece listed several of my charitable efforts that had nothing to do with the award, and it was upsetting to me.

Then there were the items that were simply cruel. In particular, the "Sound-Off" section of the local paper ran some remarks that genuinely affected me through their vindictive tones.

"Sound-Off" was a precursor of what we know today as a forum or a message board, where people could call in anonymously, share whatever was on their minds about current events, and the newspaper would print selected comments. There were some nice people who offered supportive good wishes, for which I was very grateful; however, one participant said something that cut me deeply enough that I clipped the segment from the paper and saved it.

The heading read "Mummy," and the comment included references to my husband, calling him a "mummified gorilla" and telling him to "get a life." Then the participant took me to task for keeping my job, therefore denying a job to someone who really needed it, asking, "What is wrong with these people?"

I kept the clipping because it expressed, in a nutshell, the reasons I was having so much trouble adjusting to my new life. It was wholly reflective of the attitudes I was encountering - a life lesson in a single, simple paragraph. It was more than I ever wanted to know about human nature, but I had to deal with it anyway. I discovered that I was ill equipped to do so.

Hanging on to my sense of self was a two-steps-forward, one-step-back kind of thing. I would start off a day optimistic, ready to get out into the world, go to work and to school, and take care of business. The same things I'd always done. But then someone would remind me that I was rich now, which meant I was different and I should be living like rich people live. Sometimes they implied that I had an actual *obligation* to do so. I was no longer a part of my former world, so I certainly was not welcomed there - but I didn't want to leave it, so I would tumble into confusion and anger again.

In spite of all the problems we once had, I wanted to remain the person I had always been; but now, I was the butt of jokes, the target of insults, and I'd lost so many friends that I was always waiting for the next one to fall away.

Then I would understand - or better put, remember - the burdens that might be driving these people, and I'd get centered again, grateful beyond words for the friends who stayed around. Eventually, I learned to protect myself by simply not reading, not listening, or tuning out anything that threatened my peace, which helped to some degree. But I longed for someone to talk with about my own problems and how and why I was withdrawing, because I was turning into an emotional recluse. I sometimes felt like *I* was the one who was gradually becoming mummified.

It just seemed that with most people, I wasn't allowed to *have* any burdens; in essence, they seemed to think that lots of money somehow had the power to wipe out any and every negative thing that could happen.

Actually, I think the same thing happens in other situations, too. There's a dynamic that often develops when we encounter someone who has something we want. The more we want it, the more our sense of injustice kicks in - like God Himself is playing favorites, and it strikes us as unfair. The result is division, much like a case of sibling rivalry will create resentment towards the "favored" one, the one who's perceived as being so blessed that they have no right to complain about anything. Ever. When you're the one who's regarded in that way, you feel buried alive, out in the cold, like you're frozen out of relationships by virtue of your bank balance.

People don't seem to understand that the only way money can keep you warm is if you burn it.

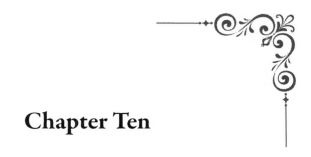

Chapter Ten

E ver since the day we deposited that first installment check from the Lottery Bureau, I'd made a habit of giving away as much as I could, every chance I got. I believed in my heart that maybe there really was something wrong with the excessive amount of money we had. It was simply too much. I felt like I owed reparations to the world, that I needed to make amends, and that I had to prove I wasn't greedy and selfish. It made absolutely no sense to me that I was given so much while others suffered.

I would look for the people who struggled silently, keeping my ears open to pick up on opportunities to help. I was especially drawn to those who wouldn't dream of asking a stranger for help. Sometimes it would be a person I knew; other times, I would hear about someone's needs through sheer coincidence.

For example, I learned about Holly's desperate situation from a friend-of-a-friend, who told me that the young mother was in danger of losing her home. Her husband had suddenly taken ill a few weeks earlier, was unable to return to work for at least six months, so Holly was scrambling to find a job to support him and her three children - one of whom was still quite small, and had been at home full-time with her. To make matters worse, it was a very tight job market back then. The price of daycare was going to wipe them out even if she was able to secure a job.

At the time, you could gift someone up to ten thousand dollars tax-free, so that's what I did. I couldn't wait to get the check to her. There was something uniquely joyful about picturing her little family with a huge burden off their shoulders, gathering around the dinner table with good food to eat and sleeping soundly in a warm house. It felt like I was breathing a sigh of relief with them.

Then there was the teenager I brought into our home, a young woman I met through a mutual friend. She had arrived at the point where she needed to leave her parents' house and get her life in order. Naturally, I was worried about it at first. She needed a lot more than just money, and I wasn't confident in my abilities to reach into her life and help her restructure it.

It went well, even better than I'd hoped for. She was a hard worker, and very responsible; today, she's a successful businesswoman who is very much in charge of her own life. I like to think I played some part in that. I hope I did.

There was also one very special couple whom I met in Las Vegas. I think Lori and Elmer wound up having a far greater impact on my life than I had on theirs. We met in a Bingo hall, where they invited me to join them - out of the blue, with no reason to include me other than the fact that I was alone and they wanted to befriend me. That evening was the beginning of a seventeen-year friendship, wherein Elmer became a close friend and Lori was almost like a second mom to me. I visited them frequently, taking them to nice restaurants and popular shows. After Elmer passed on, I would fly Lori out to see me, letting her indulge her passion for the ocean. It was an unexpected, beautiful friendship that sustained me through many difficult times. When she passed away, the loss was as painful as my mom's passing was.

Of course, I had and will always have a soft spot for hard-working people, in particular anyone who works in the service industry. I like to leave massive tips for them, then do my best to disappear before they can thank me, because that embarrasses me to no end. I've often paid anonymously for strangers' purchases at varying stores, something I started doing shortly after the lottery win. When possible, I would hide around a corner or behind a display so I could watch their reactions. As much as I enjoyed it in the early days, I always felt a little hollow afterwards, thinking I could have done more.

So I helped build the Lena Lahey Community Center, named for my mother, in my old neighborhood in Methuen. I helped establish *Girls, Inc.* in Manchester, New Hampshire, and then I worked in the kitchen there every week.

To me, it never seemed to be enough. Don't misunderstand: I have no regrets about the assistance I gave to others or the good times I shared with friends; actually, those moments make up some of my warmest memories. I hope the money I donated made a real and lasting difference in the lives around me, and that old friends remember me fondly, just as I remember them. I would do it all again in a heartbeat.

But eventually, I came to understand that my efforts would *never* be adequate. Not by my standards, anyway, and I was wearing myself out by trying to prove something - to myself, more than anyone else. I wanted to prove that I wasn't a spoiled person, unjustly enriched in a world of urgent need. I wasn't a greedy, wicked woman who had everything and shared nothing. I *wasn't* selfish and uncaring.

You can't prove a negative, though, and I was exhausted from trying. As committed as I was to doing the right thing, I wanted my motivation to help others to come from my concern and caring for them, not because I was trying to purchase some kind of relief from my guilt.

And I wanted to relax a little. Every time I set out to have fun, I would pull back, withdrawing inside the notion that I was unworthy of what I had and I needed to make it right.

It took a long time, but it finally became clear that if I was going to hang on to my identity, I needed to stop punishing myself - for lots of things - and finally figure out who and what I really was.

I also decided that while I got better acquainted with myself, I would try to have some fun.

Chapter Eleven

One of my best memories - a real *moment*, if you know what I mean - was the first time I went shopping after the win. Not for groceries or essentials of any kind, and we're not talking about discount stores or second-hand shops here: I grabbed a friend and we went to the *mall*.

I wanted to buy something just because I could, but my pre-shopping enthusiasm waned quickly. Everything I looked at was so incredibly expensive. The window shopping itself was a lot of fun, but it was difficult to find anything that I actually wanted.

After an hour or so, we wound up at one of the anchor stores. I thought I should at least apply for a credit card; after all, I was confident that I had the income for it. But when the keypad prompted me to enter my annual income, I tried to enter the amount of my annual check from the lottery... And it denied me credit. Yes, I was pretty surprised at first, wondering how much income a person actually needed to qualify for a simple box store credit card. As it turned out, the machine wouldn't recognize any amount over $999,999.99. It was an automatic rejection.

We had a good laugh over that. After that day, I would occasionally reapply for credit at different spots just to show a friend what would happen. It was a good way to poke some fun at myself, the big lottery winner who couldn't even get a credit card. It was almost like a coping mechanism. Besides, it was hilarious.

I was still driving my old car, wearing my old clothes, and I wound up returning to my usual discount stores. I was so much more comfortable in those places. I kept hearing that I needed to go to that famous street in Boston, Newbury Street, where all the fancy shops were located, but it just didn't interest me.

Then Bill decided it was time for me to have something nice, so he bought me a beautiful diamond watch, which at six hundred dollars was the most expensive piece of jewelry I'd ever owned. I loved it. It was definitely easier to accept a gift than it was to buy myself something.

But I did indulge in some wonderfully memorable excursions, in particular the trips that satisfied my obsession with football. I'm a devoted fan, an infatuation that began in the late 1960's after I read a book about the sport, and I fell in love with the New England Patriots. Actually, my passion dates all the way back to when they were the Boston Patriots back in the seventies. I had season tickets even back then, following them around with a devotion that would probably almost qualify me as a "groupie" in today's vernacular. I suppose you could say I was Patriots when Patriots wasn't cool, because they were quite the reliable losers back in those days.

Other than helping my children and getting out of debt, the best, most enjoyable thing about winning the lottery is that I've been able to attend every one of their Super Bowls since 2001, collecting enough memorabilia to create a "Patriots Shrine" in the family room of my house. In it are programs, posters, signed footballs, and a jersey signed by Tom Brady himself; however, my most prized items are all about Doug Flutie. He's one of my all-time favorite players.

I was able to go to London twice to watch the Patriots play, even had the opportunity to fly on the same jet with them. They were dressed in business attire, looking vastly different than they do in their uniforms, and they were *so* polite. On one of the trips, I dropped a few coins from my pocket as we filed out of the plane, and one of the players noticed. He held up the line while he picked them up and gave them back to me. It may seem like a small gesture, but it left an indelible impression on me.

As an aside, my pick for the best Super Bowl ever: it's a toss-up between Super Bowl XLIX and Super Bowl LI. I was there for both of them, screaming until I lost my voice. You know that meme about Tom Brady? It's the one that has a picture of him looking tough and very determined, and has the top caption of, *Dude, you need a field goal, two touchdowns, and two Two-Point Conversions. It's impossible.* Then the bottom caption says, *Hold my beer.* That was about Super Bowl LI, but it was exactly the atmosphere of both of those games. No one was giving up or giving in, and it was like Brady was able to draw on the energy of the fans to pull off the wins. It was thrilling.

By the way, if you're reading this in Atlanta or Seattle... My condolences.

Another wonderful memory was our first holiday season with no money problems. We went a bit overboard, especially for my granddaughter. We spoiled her rotten, and we loved every minute of it. None of us had ever before had a Christmas like that.

We were all together in the new house, and we had a beautiful tree and lots of presents, including two larger-than-life statues of The Blues Brothers that I got for Bill. I can't imagine what the neighbors must have thought as I brought Jake and Elwood into the house.

I cooked the traditional three-roast Christmas dinner that my mom always made for Christmas, with all the trimmings. I loved preparing a holiday in my new, modern kitchen, then serving it on my beautiful new plates. I'd never had that experience before. It was as close to the dream I'd had as a girl, of the sparkling lights and the happy faces, as I would ever get.

I did think about Mom a lot, how nice it would have been to share that time with her. I like to think that her spirit, free to go wherever she wanted to be, was right there smiling upon us. Loving us as we would always love her. I believe things like that do happen, especially at

Christmas. I thought about my dad, too, with the sad realization that he'd likely had no holiday memories to cherish. They had gotten lost inside his alcoholism.

Other than spoiling the kids and accommodating my football habit, Bill and I finally loosened up enough to take a few more trips and buy a vacation home in Las Vegas. I'm not big on gambling, but I like Vegas, and it was nice to have a regular home to live in when we went there. It was a very pretty house: a detached condo, with two bedrooms and really no yard to speak of. The community was a gated one, which made me a bit uncomfortable; however, it was close to the places we wanted to see. It was also close to some very famous people.

Not long after we moved in for our first vacation there, I found out that Wayne Newton lived not too far from us. Of course, I was quite excited at first. I couldn't wait to tell my friends, until the time came when I would have the opportunity to do that - and the words stuck in my throat. It felt awful. It felt pretentious, and phony, and I remember thinking, *Who cares? How does that define you? Does having a famous neighbor make you a more valuable person?*

So I didn't bring it up. A friend asked me once if I had ever seen Mr. Newton, and I said, "Yes, and I was surprised that it cost only $49.95. He put on quite a wonderful show."

Being Mr. Newton's neighbor was the catalyst to my first experience in name-dropping, which is something I never dreamed I would be in the position to do, and I wasn't at all prepared to handle it gracefully. But it was definitely another life lesson, and yet another opportunity to reassess my own values. The culture in the late 1990's was changing much faster than most of us in my generation could adapt to, and I sometimes found myself surprised by how often my resolve to remain unaffected was challenged. That first unexpected brush with a luminary, and my starry-eyed reaction to it, definitely got my attention.

When you think about the importance that is assigned to celebrity, you have to wonder why we seem to place such a premium on being "known." What is it about famous people that so fascinates us? I've spent a good amount of time considering that question, especially with the current culture being one of both real and manufactured fame - and I think maybe it has something to do with the fact that through their prominence, we can see them, but they can't see *us*. I mean, was I really all that impressed by seeing people like Wayne Newton in person, or was I excited by the fact that they could see *me*?

The novelty of it dissipated quickly, and we moved on to other adventures. We went on a cruise, then finally made it back to Disney. I had taken my mom and the rest of my family there before, in 1985, after four years of saving every possible penny for the trip. I have to tell you, that 1985 vacation - working so hard for so long, planning and dreaming, and then the joy of seeing Disney for the first time - seemed to mean a lot more to me than going there after the lottery win. I mean, it was great to be able to just pick up and go, but I think I appreciated it so much more back then. There's just something about the pride you feel after working hard toward a dream that you make into a reality.

I think that's one of the main reasons why I wouldn't quit my job. It's also the reason I wouldn't drop out of college. When I first started at NECC years earlier, it seemed like it might be impossible, working full time days and going to school nights while still taking care of my family. Not to mention, the cost at the time was prohibitive. But once I started taking classes, there was no way I was going to leave it behind. I'd worked hard for it, and besides, college was the most familiar and comforting thing going on in my life at the time.

The first year after the win had passed by - much of it in a blur, to be honest - and now, we were finally getting used to our new normal.

Without the distraction of the adjustment period, it soon became clear that what Bill and I had was a new life with the same old problems.

Chapter Twelve

My husband and I had gotten along pretty well throughout our marriage, partially because we weren't cemented to each other. With our opposite schedules, we shared a home and parts of our lives together, but we'd each always gone our own way and done our own thing. To my surprise, he and my mother eventually grew fond of each other. She did her part by staying out of any conflicts we had, and Bill was a loving son-in-law who was really quite kind and attentive to her.

Overall, he was a very good man; but he had a troubled past, having emerged from a broken family and then running a little wild in his youth. After we married, he retained some of his lifestyle from when he was single, going out with his friends and frequenting the bars; however, I had my interests, too - like my Thursday night Bingo and my bowling league - so we pretty much came and went as we pleased with no questions asked.

I trusted in our marriage, I suppose a little too much. I suspect that my upbringing, where I learned the value of selective naiveté, led me to turn a blind eye to the warning signs I should have noticed.

He'd made some poor choices that landed us in bad situations, especially concerning the debt we had landed in. I don't know if I was too trusting or simply naïve, but it took me a while to take serious notice of the changes in him after the lottery win. He was gambling more, I knew that because I was often with him when he gambled. And I wondered at times if now that he was rich, he was developing a roving eye. After all, he had the cash to attract other women and the means to go find them.

Regardless, we went on with our lives together. I enjoyed the relief of the routine that was returning to us after the difficult adjustment period. It sometimes seemed like we were back to being our old selves again. At least, that's what I told myself; however, the truth was that I'd lost some of my trust in him after the fiasco of our near financial ruin. But since both of us seemed relatively satisfied with our relationship, I didn't see a need to rock the boat.

Even though we were settled in, there was still one more thing I wanted to do. It was a private wish, a reverie that had played in the back of my mind for years. I wanted to find a haven. I longed for a place where I could go just to dream, and plan, and maybe retreat when I felt like the world was closing in. I wanted to own a house at the beach.

I remember the moment when I realized that I was actually going to do it. The decision came over me suddenly, during an afternoon at Salisbury Beach as I stared out at the horizon, listening to the cawing of the seagulls and feeling the ocean lap over my bare feet. It was an incredible thought, that I had the means to buy my own little refuge from the world right there, right where I wanted to be. I think there was a part of me that already knew I would need it at some point, probably very soon.

I bought my cottage on Salisbury Beach in 1998, planning on spending every May through October there. It was a small house, right on the water, with the bonus of a pool in the back - a necessity for swimmers at Salisbury, since the ocean waters there rarely break sixty degrees. It was a dream come true for me, something I had wished for ever since I was a little girl, when we would spend a couple of weeks every summer at our big family gathering at the ocean.

Bill wasn't as enamored with the beach as I was, but he would join me at the cottage every now and then during the months that I stayed there. We'd share a few days together, then he would go back to New

Hampshire. I found that too often, I was grateful to regain my solitude; but at the time, I wouldn't acknowledge that and I wouldn't think about what it meant. Whether it was due to fear, fatigue, or maybe just a sense of fatalistic self-preservation, I didn't want to confront the fact that something had gone very wrong in our marriage.

It was an aversion that was familiar to me, since I'd learned early on how to avoid problems for which I couldn't effect a solution. I knew how to construct a life around them, keeping them on the periphery of my conscious thoughts and trudging forward. The difference now was that I'd landed in a place I'd never known before: a place that was *mine*. I had dreamed it, during the lean years and through the chaotic times, and the dream had come true.

More than that, I was a busy person. A tutor at NECC, who was helping me survive Algebra, asked me why I didn't try for a full Associate Degree instead of earning only the twenty-four credits for my job and then walking away. With the unattended mess that my personal life had become, my initial reaction was one of doubt; however, that lasted less than a day. I was intrigued by the idea that a degree, something I'd never before considered because of the costs involved, was now something I could have. I started going full-time to NECC during the day and working at the IRS at night. At this point, the Y2K project I was in charge of was in full swing, so I always had plenty to do.

Being so busy helped with the tension that was building at home, but it didn't help enough. So in 1999, I became involved in The Miss New Hampshire Scholarship Program. A friend that I met at one of my Bingo games told me he was starting a pageant that year, then asked me for a donation. He seemed to be hoping for as much as fifty dollars, but when he explained that it was a scholarship-based program that would benefit young women seeking higher education, I wrote him a check for a lot more than that. He was so grateful that he asked me to join the team as a producer, which meant I would be attending the pageant... Which meant that I had to buy a formal dress.

Yeah. I was totally clueless about where and how to do that.

I asked one of my teachers at the college, an accounting professor who had become a friend and was a really sharp dresser, and he referred me to that street I'd heard so much about: Newbury Street, in Boston.

The following Saturday, I donned my customary jeans and sweatshirt, shunned my morning coffee - since I was already plenty jittery - and made the drive to Newbury Street and its seemingly endless trail of high-end shops. I'd heard the names before, seen them in the pricey magazines I leafed through while I waited in line at the grocery store, but I had no idea what I was doing there.

So I headed for the first shop I saw. I tried to pull the door open - no luck. Then I tried to push it, but it seemed to be locked. I stepped back, confused, because I could see a few people in there and they didn't exactly look like the janitorial crew, if you know what I mean.

A woman stepped in front of me and a buzzer went off, and she was able to open the door quite easily. I shrugged and followed her inside.

Two of the sales people noticed me, their expressions quickly shifting from alarm to a kind of a closed-off indifference. They hurried over to me and one of them asked, "Did we have a booking for you?"

A booking?

"Uh, no..." I answered weakly. I didn't even know what she was talking about. I thought that most stores *wanted* people to come in and buy their stuff.

"I'm sorry, ma'am, but we require an appointment," she said.

She certainly didn't sound sorry. Her tone was actually quite intimidating. I remember thinking that she would have made a terrific high school principal.

She managed somehow to maneuver me to the door without having to touch me. "We sell haute couture here, so of course, viewing is by appointment only," she explained.

Her cohort was nodding, chiming in with, "There wouldn't be anything here that would..." After an awkward silence, she finished with, "... be of any interest to you."

Suddenly, I had a brief déjà vu moment.

I thought, *Didn't I see this in a movie once?*

Anyway, I made a beeline out the door. It was so embarrassing. I chided myself for being naïve. Ignorant. In my mind's eye, I saw myself as a new-money transplant into a world I didn't belong to and didn't want to inhabit. I was from Methuen, for pity's sake. I used words like "tonic" when others said "soda." I put an "r" at the end of words where it didn't belong, and for the life of me couldn't pronounce an "r" where it *did* belong.

I cringed a little, remembering how in my generation, the upper crust would refer to people like me as "common."

When that word started playing around in the back of my mind, I felt something rising up within me, and it felt good - like my self-respect was finally rearing up on its hind legs and getting loud. Okay, sure. I was average. A regular person. The "common" kind, even.

An average, regular, totally common woman... With a net worth of forty-two million dollars, which that store would not be benefiting from.

There were very few times throughout the years that I allowed the fact of the money to comfort me in that way, because I didn't want to succumb to "putting on airs," which is another of my generation's sayings. No one's worth is measured by a bank balance, in spite of what people like the women in that store believed, and rising above that kind of bias is a simple choice. It's an easy one to make, because pretension is a quality so shallow you can simply step out of it.

But I have to be honest: finding out later that those sales people worked on commission did make me smile for a moment. *Only* for a moment. Seriously.

After taking a few minutes to regroup, and to work through my sudden impulse to get in my car and escape back to New Hampshire, I wandered down the famous, seemingly unwelcoming Newbury Street. I ducked into the next place that had something in the window that I liked, ascertaining first that there were other people going inside without waiting for a buzzer to grant them entry. I'd already decided that if the people in this store told me that I wasn't their kind of customer, I'd head back home and hit up Target on my way there.

They didn't. They were actually quite nice and very understanding, even supportive of the fact that I was completely out of my element. I left with an exquisite outfit for the pageant. It was the first extravagant piece of formalwear I'd ever owned: a suit with soft, flowing pants and a glittery gold top with a matching jacket. I bought shoes, too. I indulged in a pair of gold pumps with a smooth satin lining and a small heel.

I must admit, putting that outfit on created something of a change in my outlook. I'd never been one for glitzing myself up with fancy clothes and such, because I always believed - and still do - that the person inside is what's important. With that said, I began to appreciate the boost I got from wrapping that inner person in a nicer package.

It was a much-needed enhancement to my confidence, especially as I was embarking on the new venture with the Miss New Hampshire Program, which was a truly inspiring experience. So much so, that I remain involved with the pageant to this day, as both Field Director and state treasurer.

Even with staying busy, I kept getting the uneasy feeling that a day of reckoning was coming between Bill and me. When the Y2K project wrapped up, school settled down, and the pageant system hit its off-season, the day arrived.

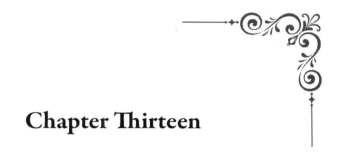

Chapter Thirteen

I sometimes asked myself why I didn't confront Bill sooner, but I knew why.

Although I was aware that something was going on behind my back, I've never been able to feel jealousy. It's like I didn't inherit the green-eyed gene or something, because I don't even understand that feeling. It strikes me as being the embodiment of humiliation, of chasing down one's own loss of dignity. Maybe it's just my pragmatic bent, but I figure that if someone wants to stray, if they're determined to betray their promises, then they will. There's nothing you can do to contain a heart that wants to be somewhere else.

In 2001, right around Bill's birthday, I went into his office and found a note with a woman's name and phone number on it. For some reason, that note got me thinking, and I couldn't shake it off. My thoughts finally led me to confront the truths that I had been hiding from. Somehow, I just *knew*.

After spending so much time and energy trying to avoid reality, it arrived with a flurry of sudden memories - snippets of moments that cascaded over my mind like a game of 52-Pickup, creating a clear picture for me as I retrieved them and put them in order. I thought about the late nights that became days-long disappearances, the missing money, the phone calls he would receive that I wasn't allowed to overhear.

The final thing I had to acknowledge was how unwelcome I felt in his life. On that day, I finally let it in.

I took some time to myself to regain my emotional footing; then, when I did make an issue of it, Bill did the one thing that could end my relationship with him. He lied. As unaffected as I am by jealousy, I'm equally distraught when faced with a liar. Of course, no one enjoys being openly lied to, but brazen deception by a loved one is one of the few things that will shut me down.

That's what happened, and it happened quickly. The confrontation wasn't anything that even resembled a blowup; actually, our emotional parting was calm to the point of being almost resigned in nature, like it was a foregone conclusion of some kind. But now, I knew the truth. In facing it directly, I allowed it to become my reality.

I stopped loving him that day. Although we didn't physically split up right away, it seemed that standing by him for so many years, dealing with the endless problems while trying to hold some semblance of a life together, had drained me. I felt like I was simply exhausted. It had been too much for too long.

For all intents and purposes, we were living entirely separate existences after that, and life - in spite of having developed a serious limp - went on. It was so stressful, though, living divided in the same home. There was something achingly empty about every moment I spent in the lake house in New Hampshire. The rooms I'd designed, the furnishings I'd so carefully picked, even the wall of family pictures that stared out at me - it hurt to look at all of it. It felt very much like a mockery. I still missed the friends who were gone, who had walked away and never looked back. And the fact that my mother, the only person who had ever loved me unconditionally, had so recently left me... It was all getting to be too heavy to carry around anymore.

I remember opening my desk drawer one day and finding pictures of my birthday party the year before. My fiftieth. Danielle had called me at six a.m. to tell me to rise, shine, and enjoy my birthday to the fullest. It was a prank to wake me up, since she knew I'm not at all a morning person.

I was relaxing at home, playing with my granddaughter Izzy, just enjoying a quiet day - when all of a sudden, I heard cars honking. I looked out the window and saw a caravan of vehicles coming down the driveway. Bill and Danielle had arranged a surprise party for me.

The guests came streaming in to the house, which wasn't at all prepared for a gathering of any kind; however, they had apparently been planning it for weeks, which I realized when the caterers appeared and set up a wonderful buffet for everyone. One of the guests set up a karaoke machine on the deck; another friend readied a full bar in the family room. It was definitely a memorable way to celebrate my birthday. After the initial shock of it, I reveled in every moment.

That was a good day, probably my last really nice memory of the lake house. Holding those pictures in my hand, I wondered why I had so quickly gone cold toward Bill. I admitted to myself that I'd been holding on by a thread for a long time, a fact that I'd kept hidden inside my deeply-ingrained survival instincts. It was a part of my personality that I wanted to change - I just didn't know how.

While my feelings for my husband had ended as suddenly as a door slamming closed, the actual road to divorce was a long, complicated journey. During 2001, Bill and I slowly moved on to separate residences, his at the lake house in New Hampshire and mine at Salisbury Beach.

I'd already started spending more and more time at my cottage on the ocean, so it made sense to move there year-round. Sure enough, it did become my sanctuary, just like I thought it would when I bought it years earlier.

That little beach house saved my sanity. It was there that I began healing, finding the clarity of mind to begin creating the rest of my life after Bill and I decided to live apart.

After we separated, I kept working at the travel agency and going to school, while trying to care for myself and making sure I kept an eye on the kids. But I needed something. Because Bill and I were still married, I couldn't bring myself to go outside my marriage for solace, and I didn't really want to anyway. Sure, I was lonely at times, but that just isn't who I am.

I constantly felt like I was at loose ends. I blamed much of my mood on the lottery, brooding about how that one win had produced a string of losses that were starting to extract their price from my very soul. It felt like I was doing a slow-motion tumble into a pit of melancholy, one that I wasn't always adverse to, and my indifference scared me.

I knew I needed to turn myself around, and fast.

One of my favorite things to do was to take long walks along the shore, breathing in the sea air, watching the gulls spread their wings so the cool breezes would lift them toward Heaven. Were I ever to feel envy, it would be directed at those seagulls. I wanted to live like they did.

Even though I never was all that philosophical, always relying more on my analytical side, I spent a lot of time reflecting. At first, I thought a lot about happiness, how elusive it was now and had always been. Even the most joyous moments could turn on a dime, sending me into another round of doubt, self-recrimination, and a feeling like life had betrayed me.

But at some point, it occurred to me that the same is true for *all* of us. It's just part of the human condition. I eventually came to the conclusion that happiness is not something to strive for: it's simply the fleeting result of our temporal needs being met. I was searching for something more permanent, a tranquility that would sustain me in my life. Happiness is capricious, a moment-to-moment thing that is wholly dependent on circumstances - not to mention, other people - whereas serenity is a state of being. I wanted serenity.

Bit by bit, I started to take pleasure in life again, commemorating the change in my perspective with a little sign that said *Moore Fun* that I hung on the front porch. It was a statement, but it was also a reminder. I wanted to make sure that I never again allowed discouragement to bury my spirit.

I knew the key to that was quite simple, yet equally elusive: it was a commitment to truly living The Golden Rule. I needed to stay involved, live with my eyes wide open, and tend to the needs of others.

But I learned that there's a flip side to that. Yes, we need to treat people the way we hope they'll treat us; on the other hand, if they don't, then we need to care for ourselves in the ways that we wish others would.

By the end of my first full year of living at the beach, I was getting restless. It was time to rejoin the world. I was ready to get back out there, reopen my heart to new projects, new adventures, and to the small circle of friends who had stayed beside me.

Discovering who my true friends were had been both the greatest gift and the most heartbreaking aspect of that time. My gratitude for the people who loved me and saw me through everything is immeasurable.

But there was a time when my love for them was also unhealthy.

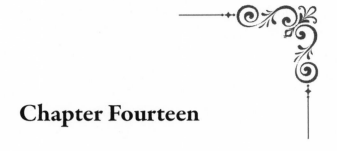

Chapter Fourteen

I was always looking for tangible ways to express my love for my friends, a need that seemed to increase after the separation from my husband, but they would brush off my attempts to share the wealth with them. Every one of them insisted that they wanted only to continue our relationship just like we were before the win. They wouldn't even let me pay for a night out at a restaurant - we always went halves on the tab or divided it equally, the same as we always had; yet there was a growing, gnawing sense of discomfort there. In spite of any resolve to remain unaffected, it was obvious that something had changed.

The problem finally revealed itself when my oldest friend, Danielle, came from Maine for a visit. Her car, which had definitely seen better days, chose that weekend to break down in a big way. The engine completely blew out.

I remember my initial reaction of alarm, but it quickly turned to delight. I could finally do something for a friend. I poured her a cup of coffee and we sat at my kitchen table to discuss her options.

"You know that you need a new car, Danielle," I said. I wanted to be gentle about it, because I knew she would resist, and she did.

Shaking her head, she answered with a simple, "No, I don't."

"Yeah, you do."

"Don't worry about it. I'll find a way to get this one fixed."

"By Sunday? You have to be back at work on Monday morning."

She looked hopeless then, and it hurt me deeply to see her like that. While I really did understand her reluctance to accept my help, we both knew that her car was a goner and she was in no position to do anything about it.

More than that, it was painful to think that even now, she wouldn't let me do a single thing to help her. I had known Danielle since high school. She'd been in my wedding. We had shared our lives with each other for over thirty years; yet there I was, with more money than I knew what to do with, and she wouldn't let me do anything at all to ease her burdens.

"Dani." I took her hand. "Please, won't you let me do this one thing for you?"

She was shaking her head again. "I don't want you to think I love you for your money. I don't want anything to change between us."

When she said that, I remember thinking, *Just that statement means things have already changed.*

"What does money have to do with it?" I asked. "We've always helped each other with whatever we had, and *that's* what's changed. You didn't even let me buy you breakfast this morning." I waited until she looked up at me. "We're friends. You would do the same for me."

"I know. It's just different now."

"No it's not. Not unless you decide it is."

My stomach was hurting, a gripping pain that was like a mixture of disappointment and loneliness, and I decided I wanted to tell her about it. I wanted her to understand how much joy I would feel in knowing she had a nice, safe car. I wanted to tell her how badly it hurt to feel separated from her needs - like I was standing on the periphery of her life, watching her suffer, and she wouldn't let me intervene.

But the only thing I could come up with was, "Don't you know how much this would *mean* to me?"

There must have been something in my voice, or maybe in my expression, that changed her mind. A long moment later, she nodded.

"Actually, I didn't know, but I think I get it now."

I exhaled then and squeezed her hand. "Then let's go car shopping," I said.

Our first stop was at a large dealership in Salem, New Hampshire, where Danielle got a first-hand look at a repeat of the Newbury Street shop that turned me away.

I told the salesman that my friend needed a new car, and I would pay full price in cash if they could have it ready by Sunday.

He glanced at my outfit - the usual sneakers and jeans - and he grinned.

"Seriously?" He smirked like he thought he was being punked, then glanced around the showroom like he was looking for the cameras or something. "You want a brand-new car, ready by Sunday, and you'll just pull the money out of your purse?"

"Something like that."

"Okay. Sure, ladies. I'll get right on it."

He was shaking his head, laughing as he walked away, and Danielle turned to me with her mouth hanging open.

"Oh my gosh, Paula. Did he really just blow us off?" she asked.

"It's happened before," I sighed, and then I told her about my adventure at the boutique on Newbury Street. We had a good chuckle over it as we left.

The salesman at the next dealership was quite thrilled to sell us a car. I explained the situation to him, adding that the store just down the street had laughed at me, then asking him if he wanted to take the sale the other guy threw away.

"It will be my absolute pleasure, Ms. Moore," he assured me, and Danielle and I spent a few very enjoyable hours finding the perfect car for her.

As she drove off that Sunday, honking the horn and waving, I felt a massive weight lifting from my shoulders. More than the relief that she finally had a safe, reliable mode of transportation - her car had been an issue for a long time - it seemed to me that we'd overcome something that had the potential to damage our friendship.

She had been excessively careful to avoid any appearance of wanting me in her life for my money, to the point that she was shutting me out; I, on the other hand, had been so concerned about denting her pride that I was actually afraid to offer her something she desperately needed.

I was also afraid of losing her, and it was a huge, demoralizing shock to confront that part of myself. I'd become so cautious, so anxious to hang on to the friends I still had - and yes, so mistrusting of even my long-term, closest relationships - that I was willing to stand aside and let loved ones direct the course of our lives together, sometimes even to their detriment. And mine.

I can't truthfully say I completely changed my entire perspective after that day. It would take me years to adjust to all of the changes, the most distressing of which was the end of my marriage. But the experience of suddenly living on my own was also an amazingly freeing thing. It was the catalyst to the most pronounced and rewarding growth of my life. I learned how to let go.

It took me a long time to fully understand the reasons for and consequences of hanging on too tightly, and allowing fear to take priority over love. I recently heard a relationship guru on the internet or TV or someplace, talking about how love and fear can't coexist, that they're mutually exclusive, so you function through either one or the other. I thought that as astute as he seemed to be, he was misled, and he had the platform with which to mislead others.

In my opinion, you can never know genuine fear unless and until you love someone - and when you do, you lose your sense of autonomy. Your perceptions, your optimism, and your peace of mind are dependent on the safety and security of another, yet those good feelings will exist only if they make choices over which you have no control. Is there anything more frightening than that?

That's why it is within these closest, most vital relationships that we can make our costliest mistakes. It's also where we learn our most valuable lessons.

Part Two

The first few years after the win were fraught with difficult readjustments, and that time was very much like an odyssey: by necessity, I had to acknowledge and then incorporate the changes in my life, as well as accept and then deal with the things that had never changed and never would.

I saw both the best and the worst of human nature. The best was witnessing the resilience of heroic people whose existences revolved around their loved ones. I learned from them, and I take their strength with me in my life. I hope I gave something back to them, or at least to the world around me in their stead.

Through the worst, I learned more than anything else the hard lessons of forgiveness. I found out that I had to confront and then fully address my own unforgiving nature, including toward myself.

I'm in my mature years now, a senior citizen who lives in a little house in a nice neighborhood in New Hampshire. The checks have stopped, something that is actually a great relief to me. I recently retired, so now I spend my days with my friends, or traveling, or doing a little gardening before having dinner and watching my favorite TV shows. While I'm still actively involved in my projects like Miss New Hampshire, mine is a wonderfully quiet and uncomplicated life.

I never remarried. I just didn't have the desire to do so. When I was first getting used to living alone, I worried at times about growing old by myself. I was certain it would be a lonely experience; yet except for occasional moments of feeling somewhat isolated or misunderstood, it hasn't been very lonely at all.

Both before and after my husband and I separated, I know I made as many blunders as the next person. Probably more. But I think the greatest rewards of the past twenty years came from the lessons I learned, especially after I was out on my own.

I like to think those experiences left me with a few insights, maybe even some wisdom that is worth sharing. That's something we seniors should do more often - discuss what we know about living - because wisdom is a hard-won, intangible part of the soul that makes life rich in a way that money can't buy.

Chapter Fifteen

I n some ways, adjusting to living on my own was a bit more difficult than I thought it would be. Most people who experience the end of a marriage know the relief that the initial breakup can bring; however, once that passes and you get settled into your solitary life, you realize that there are still problems. The difference is that now, you face them by yourself.

But I found that there is a benefit to that, as well: for the first time in my life, my mistakes would be my own, because all of my choices were exactly that. Mine. I worried at first about messing up, and occasionally I was too hard on myself; but over time, I stopped fretting. I acknowledged the fact that I would make mistakes, and accepted my failings with a sense of humor. Then I would find ways to put my missteps to good use. Most surprising to me was discovering that without the pressure of a failing marriage, I was better able to focus on the things that needed my attention. It was like my mind opened up.

Bill and I still interacted on a regular basis, doing our best to keep our relationship friendly. We had children and grandchildren, and our paths often crossed within their lives; besides, we had decided to stay legally married, an arrangement that lasted for many years.

To this day, I'm not sure why I agreed to that. Although we'd gotten legal advice about our rather unusual financial situation, with the lawyers informing us that we each potentially had quite a lot to lose, I think there was a part of me that wasn't ready for a while to make it official. I regard marriage as a lifetime commitment, one that the courts can dissolve only in the realm of legalities. There's so much more to a marriage than that.

My husband and I had a complicated but workable financial arrangement, wherein I took care of all the finances and wrote him a substantial annual spousal support check for his own use. He kept the lake house in New Hampshire, I kept the cottage on Salisbury Beach. We divided our material possessions and went our separate ways.

The irony of the situation was not lost on me, though. The same money that I believe enabled, even accelerated the demise of our marriage was also a factor in keeping us legally wed for years after the marriage was functionally over.

I had always considered myself to be relatively self-reliant, so I was sure I could manage life very well on my own. I was still running the travel agency, still involved with projects like Miss New Hampshire, and I was thinking about returning to college for my Bachelor's Degree in Business Administration. I believed I was quite capable to handle whatever issues arose in life.

Right up until the day that my hot water heater broke down.

Finding a technician to replace it was an easy process, but finding one who didn't treat me like I was teetering on the brink of senility was another matter. I think many women, especially those of us who have reached our mature years, are often talked down to by repair people. In my case, I experienced an additional dynamic going on, one that happened often enough that I called it "The Robin Hood Effect." There were times when a contractor found out that I was *that* Paula Moore; and suddenly, the problem I hired them to fix would become a lot more complicated than they initially said, and their rates would increase substantially. It seemed to me that they regarded me as an elderly woman who was too stupid to realize she was being ripped off by them - and since I was wicked rich, they felt they were somehow entitled to do all they could to transfer the wealth.

Of course, they were right about one thing: I was not educated in most aspects of the highly technical work these people can do. What they didn't understand was the fact that a lack of education is in no way the same thing as a lack of intelligence.

When the situation became clear to me, I decided I would learn a new craft: home repair and maintenance. I didn't don a pair of overalls and a tool belt; instead, I educated myself on the basics, so I was better able to spot a scam if one appeared.

It wasn't so much my angst over the money that got me learning how to take care of my own needs. It was that insecure, anxious feeling of being so entirely dependent on others to keep my life up and running. And the determination to row my own boat extended well beyond my hot water heater. Being patronized by people of superior knowledge, which at times had included those who dealt in both legal and money matters, helped me make the decision to go for a higher degree. After several disastrous incidents of getting bad direction from people whom I trusted to advise me, based on their level of expertise, I decided to dig in and get myself informed.

This remains a huge issue to me, because there are so many women in my generation who are on their own, and far too many of them find themselves at the mercy of a technician, an expert, or a specialist. Better said, they *believe* that to be the case - that they have no power, and therefore no choices.

Don't get me wrong: I know that there are countless highly skilled professionals out there who build their businesses on the rock of their own integrity. I've met them, I've hired them, and I refer others to them. Yet I believe that people in general, and women in particular, need to enlighten themselves in areas that have traditionally been thought of as the exclusive domain of specialists. Of all the changes I adapted to, it was educating myself on the everyday challenges of life that gave me the most pride, and resulted in an immeasurable boost to my confidence.

A certain amount of self-reliance is an essential component of human dignity, something that has no relation to income or social standing and is sorely lacking in this culture. It's a complicated problem that in my opinion is contributing to the chaos in our world. I believe that dignity is based on the cultivation and development of two personal attributes: education and self-respect.

The process of educating ourselves can be as simple as opening a book, logging onto the internet, or seeking advice from someone whose experience surpasses our own. But getting a formal education - earning a college degree that will open doors to a career and a better life - that's an entirely different thing. More than any other factor, the costs involved put it out of the reach of too many people.

In my own experience, I grew up knowing that I would never be able to afford to go to college, especially on my own nickel. My parents had very little money, so of course, they couldn't help; yet my longing for a college degree was a dream that I had a great deal of trouble letting go of.

My fascination with business kept building, though. Back in my high school days, students could pick from any of three different career paths for their studies. One of them was General Ed, for those who didn't perform well in school or who simply didn't know what they wanted to do with their lives. There was also Business, which is the one I picked, since I knew what I wanted but also knew I couldn't go to college. It was the only choice available to me, because the last track was College Prep, and college was an unattainable dream for me.

I believe that generally speaking, women are especially vulnerable to being held down and held back by lacking a college degree. Even if they are willing and able to go thousands of dollars into debt, they usually have responsibilities that take priority over their desire to go to college. I knew women who were in those situations, which is why I created the endowment at Northern Essex Community College; however, I took small comfort from doing that. My contribution is a drop in the bucket when compared to the extensive and ongoing need.

I don't take my ability to go to college for granted. Ever. I enjoyed the challenges of furthering my education, and other than Algebra, I did pretty well. I especially liked the feeling of being pushed to learn. Eventually, it became something of an obsession.

But if not for winning the lottery, it's likely that I would have ended my studies at my Associate Degree, if not sooner; and to me, that fact is a very sad commentary on the issue of affordable learning. Although I'm not an advocate for government-funded, free education for everyone, I do think we could benefit from policies that would deregulate the education industry. Perhaps addressing the barriers put up by over-regulation would have the effect of opening up the market for new and innovative ideas.

In my opinion, when you lack education, your self-esteem suffers. You often have to rely on others to do *for* you, instead of doing for yourself, and that breeds a sense of helplessness and dependency that destroys self-respect.

At this point in our history, we have a culture that is fast devolving into one of unquestioned entitlement, which is the opposite of dignity. Perhaps we can attribute a portion of that to a lack of education; then again, the most heroic and dignified people I've ever known were usually the ones who, in spite of their difficult situations, asked for nothing. They kept their eyes straight ahead and charted their own course.

If anything, some of the most entitled folks I've ever met showed up in my life with lofty titles, important positions, advanced degrees, and abundant chutzpa. Still others were members of my personal inner circle, whose greed overrode the better parts of their souls. Those were the people who disappointed me the most.

Unfortunately, it's an attitude I confronted many times over the last twenty years.

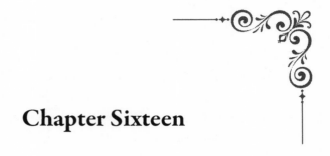

Chapter Sixteen

Since I had won the lottery on St. Patrick's Day, I made an annual event out of gifting the special people in my life money on that date. I would take them out to a celebratory meal at a nice restaurant to give them each a check, thinking they would put the money to good use. It made me happy, imagining their lives getting easier, picturing them planning for the future and enjoying life a little more while they did so.

I never once indicated to anyone that the money would come every year, like clockwork, for the full twenty years that I received lottery payments. Actually, I thought I was exceedingly careful to let them all know that they would get their gifts until they were in a more secure and more stable position in life, and better able to work toward their dreams.

Yet again, I saw how money changes people. I used to scoff at the cynical notion that "no good deed goes unpunished." I don't anymore.

For example, there was the situation where I gifted one family several times, until they had enough money to put a substantial down payment on a house. I was quite pleased with that, thinking about how wonderful it would be for them to have their own home. Yet the first year that I didn't call them for the annual St. Patrick's Day dinner, they contacted me and demanded to know why there was no check for them that year.

That was discouraging enough; however, when I explained to them again that I had never intended to continue giving out checks for the whole twenty years, they walked out of my life and never spoke to me again.

There were others who would use the money for less-than-healthy purposes. When I found out about these indiscretions, of course I didn't want to help them hurt themselves or their families, so I stopped giving them gifts. They, too, discarded me when they realized I wasn't going to change my mind about that.

I can't truthfully say that I was shocked by their behavior. I was perhaps a little surprised, definitely hurt and disappointed. I also felt guilty for a while, like I was responsible for getting them used to the extra money and then pulling it away; but by this time, I thought of myself as being accustomed to, even expectant of the ugliness that money can create in otherwise decent, loving people.

Then when I realized how blasé I was becoming toward those occurrences, it deeply troubled me. I spent a few sleepless nights wrestling with how cynical I had become. I was getting sick and tired of my own pessimism, and even more discouraged over how many of my less-than-charitable attitudes were being pointed out to me on a regular basis.

The only way I could resolve my disillusionment, as well as my disturbingly minimal reaction to it, was to come to the conclusion that you can't dictate what someone will do with a gift. But when you realize that you're funding another's demise, you can withdraw from supporting it. I believe you have a moral responsibility to do so.

Of course, it's a lot more difficult when this issue arises in your own family. I worried constantly about my children, and whether or not I was giving them too much. If I was, I feared how it would affect them. They each had lovely houses, paid in full, which is something I did for them that I will never regret. They each had beautiful, brand new cars - but that, I was a little ambivalent about. Still, I was glad that they had safe transportation.

However, I sometimes think I made a mistake in giving them jobs at Travel Anywhere, the travel agency I owned. I was able to pay them whatever salary I wanted to, and I was generous - so much so, that the IRS decided to audit me one year to make sure that ours was a legitimate employer-employee relationship. The audit was no big deal to me. In some ways, I actually enjoyed the process, because I knew we were buttoned down with all the legalities. We were completely legitimate. I was a tax professional, after all.

But in making the amount of money they made, my children had little incentive to attain a higher education. That was an unintended, unanticipated consequence that caused me a good deal of concern.

Not to say they were lazy, not at all. They were and still are two industrious, hard working young adults. With that said, it seemed like the fact that they were being well-compensated for the jobs they did at the agency had the effect of lessening their interest in going to college. I wanted to find a way to encourage them to get their degrees.

My mother had gone only as far as the 9th Grade in her schooling, a point I often raised to my children. I thought that by earning my Associate Degree, they would adopt the attitude that if Mom could do it, they could do it, too. I had minimal success with my efforts in that regard, though. They both attempted going to college, but they didn't graduate, probably because they weren't ready at the time.

So I thought I'd throw another challenge out there to them by enrolling at Merrimack College for my Bachelor's Degree. While I was there, I discovered that I was drawn to the fields of accounting and business; additionally, since I was running the travel agency at this point, the extra education came in very handy.

I still didn't get much of a rise out of my kids, though. My son earned a certificate, but that was about it. He had also learned a good amount about computers and web design during the years he worked for me. Eventually, when I closed the agency and he was out on his own, he did go back to school, earning first his Associate and then his Bachelor's degree. My daughter took various courses until she discovered what she wanted to do, and is now getting close to completing her degree. I'm glad to say that they're doing well. I'm so proud of them for the way they found their own paths in life.

For me, going back to college uncovered an unexpected passion for doing taxes, of all things. There was something about putting a return together, organizing the bits and pieces that make up someone's financial life, that was absolutely fascinating - as were the courses I took in Forensic Accounting. I knew very little about the subject when I started, but I took to it like a duck to water. My studies provided feelings of accomplishment that I got nowhere else, a rush that was much like the satisfaction you get from conquering a difficult puzzle. I wanted to go further, so I decided to go for my Master's Degree.

I was still living in my cottage at the beach back then, and I thought it would be a great way to spend my time during the cold, sometimes lonely winter months when the area was somewhat deserted. I briefly considered working toward becoming a CPA; but I felt relatively fulfilled by the time I got my Master's, as well as proud of myself for accomplishing what I had. I had gone as far as I wanted to with education. I was offered a teaching position at Northern Essex Community College, and although I was honored by that, I wasn't really looking to work for a salary anymore. Besides, I was getting ready to retire from the travel agency at this point.

After I closed Travel Anywhere, and my children were finally on their own and doing great, I would often think about whether or not the years of spoiling them served only to impede their growth and their independence. I believe it probably did, especially since they've done such a good job with their lives in the years since.

I've come to understand that the reason I kept jumping in, giving them whatever they wanted and solving their problems for them, was in part because of my guilt. It's something I do regret - a flaw in my parenting that took many years to recognize and then correct. It's to my children's credit that they were strong enough and resilient enough to overcome it, then move on to create lives they could be proud of.

I know that countless parents can say this, but they had it rough growing up. They weren't proud of the house they grew up in. I suspect there were times when they weren't proud of their family, either. In the early years, I daydreamed more often than I ever let on about giving them everything they wanted. I'm sure they never knew how often I would check on them after they were asleep at night, standing there watching them, hoping, like all mothers and fathers do, that they would somehow have a better life than their parents had.

Since I couldn't redo their childhoods, that hopefulness became a desire to give them anything and everything they wanted after I won the lottery. Like I said, buying their homes for them is something I would do again; however, I went way beyond that. Perhaps some of the excesses were due to the simple relief of knowing they would want for nothing, but I think that my own childhood of growing up with constant unmet material needs was also a contributing factor. I felt guilty, like their father and I had let them down when they were small, and I wanted to make it up to them. I wanted them to have it easier than I did.

It took me many years to realize that in removing any opportunity for them to struggle, I was risking their futures in an entirely different way, denying them the chances to develop the strength that my own mother had allowed me to find within myself. Not only was I minimizing their abilities to show the world their tenacity, but what I didn't understand at the time was that my coddling them was also the most efficient way to cripple them.

I became more and more uncomfortable with my behavior toward them as the years passed, especially as I slowly became conscious of the fact that in reality, I was disrespecting them in a very basic way. I wish I would have brought my concerns out into the open, maybe found someone to talk to about the mistakes I was making, but the practice of overindulging children fast becomes a vicious cycle: you regard them as being damaged by a past that you can't erase, therefore you think they're unable to survive without your help. And even when that's not true - as my own children have shown me - you further convince yourself, with each gift and every check, that you're right. Then you give them more to assuage your own anxiety.

Another reason I allowed all of this to continue to a crisis point was due to my own conditioning, and the idea that family problems should stay within the family. I never was one to seek any kind of help. Not because it wasn't needed, but because it never occurred to me that anyone *could* help. I was still functioning within the grim, stoic secrecy that is another one of the legacies of growing up in an addicted home. I never even mentioned my concerns to my closest friends.

I never broached the topic among acquaintances, either, even when I witnessed others engaging in similar practices with their children. And although there is a widespread notion these days that the generations coming up behind us are feckless, spoiled little "snowflakes" who can't fend for themselves - an attitude incorporating both an idea and a label that I fully reject - I don't hear many people talking about how these kids were raised. There are parenting issues that need to be acknowledged, confronted, and resolved.

It's just way too easy to wag our fingers at the young people who have trouble navigating their lives, telling them to shape up, grow up, and in essence, shut up. I think misguided, sometimes full-on bad parenting is to blame for the lion's share of their confusion.

In particular, I believe that parenting through guilt has become a huge problem. It's almost the norm in our culture, and the truth is that there are plenty of good reasons for that guilt, because we've left a terrible mess to our children. But we don't want to discuss who is responsible for the mess. We don't want to confront our failings. We'd rather belittle the results of our efforts.

When you think about the numbers of children who are trying to survive a home life that involves addiction, abuse, or indifference, and who are placated only by the power of purchase or the dismissive leniency of a distracted parent, the public scorn and ridicule that is directed at these kids is something we all should be ashamed of. Do I think that troubled children are blameless for their actions and choices? No. But two things come to mind in that regard: first, as a society, we tend to lump our young people into faceless groups like "Gen-Z" and "Millennials," which is quite convenient for the marketing purposes of corporate America, but has the effect of denying them their individuality.

Second, we need to better appreciate and encourage the success stories. Many of these kids come shining through the worst imaginable situations, doing good for both themselves and for others; however, we also need to stop the contemptuous attitudes toward those children who are struggling to make their way into a world without guard rails. We need to look at them, listen to them, and help them. After all, the very people who enjoy mocking "snowflakes" come from the generations who took a sledge hammer to those cultural guard rails - or who stood by silently while others did so.

I think back to my childhood - which, by the way, I in no way romanticize. There were more than enough societal issues to contend with in the 1950's. For example, Polio was still a very real danger, the Civil Rights Movement was only beginning to finally get some traction, and the Cold War was starting between the United States and Russia. Then in the 1960's, we went from what we now recall as a golden era to complete chaos within one decade.

The difference, however, was that we had a sense of right and wrong. We had core values that weren't defined by individuals. They weren't created by governmental bodies with an agenda, to whom we answered concerning every aspect of our lives, or corporations with a bottom line to address. Our values were created by God, and we answered to Him. Now that we've pushed God out of the culture, apparently having decided that we can run things just fine without Him, we answer to nothing but our temporal whims.

Anecdotal arguments notwithstanding, life really was better back then. It was more meaningful; certainly, it was far more hopeful. Even though we tend to idealize our youthful years, I can't imagine those whom we condescendingly refer to as "the boomerang generation" will hold such fond thoughts about their own childhoods.

When I hear people mocking and denigrating them, I think of the young people I've known. I remember the exemplary women I've met through my work with the Miss New Hampshire Scholarship Program. Their dignity and their optimism is inspirational. I have no doubt that every one of them will leave their mark on the world.

Maybe it would be more difficult to degrade the children whom *we raised* if we spent less time going from coddling them in order to buy off our collective guilt, to critiquing and criticizing them when we find that we don't like the results - and spent more time actually listening to them.

I wish I would have learned that lesson sooner, but I did come around in time to make at least some difference in the lives of the people I love the most.

Chapter Seventeen

Overall, I think my family came through everything okay. We had our problems, but most of them conquered the challenges with minimal scarring. Some of them managed to thrive, like my oldest granddaughter, Izzy. She has grown into an outstanding young woman.

I consider that itself to be a miracle, since it wasn't a foregone conclusion that she would grow up at all. Izzy, at eighteen months old, was diagnosed with a form of cancer that was very rare in a child her age; so much so, that she became a case study in the disease. Even though she was cured within a year or so, she had to endure rounds of chemotherapy and all of the problems that come with that treatment, as well as subsequent surgery to clean up the aftereffects of the cancer.

Needless to say, those were challenging days for all of us, filled with apprehension - revolving around our sometimes frantic efforts to secure not only the medications she needed, but the money to pay for them. We also worried about the possible emotional impact on Izzy, and whether or not her illness and the treatments she received would affect her throughout her life.

My daughter and I would take her to the pediatric cancer ward at a hospital in Boston. It was a dreary place back then, where Izzy was taken to a room that was very much like a closet to receive her treatments, and it was always difficult and frightening for her. But the doctors and the nurses at that place showed her a great deal of compassion, always trying to make her as comfortable as possible.

In spite of the constant sense of dread, I managed to hold every-thing together, especially my emotions - not because I'm so terrifically strong or anything, but because there really wasn't any alternative. But after Izzy was healthy again, I would often retreat into a place of spiritual quietness, wondering why she had to go through it at all. Her cancer seemed like a capricious turn of events, a trauma that had no meaning, and I was one who always sought the deeper meaning in all things. The world needed to make sense to me. Watching my baby granddaughter battle cancer, absolutely nothing made sense.

It wasn't a lessening of my faith, not at that point: it was more like an existentialistic resignation to the human condition. I thanked God that she was cured, and I meant it; however, I also began contemplating who He is in ways that I hadn't before. I simply couldn't understand. Not yet.

So I focused my gratitude on those who helped us through our trials, especially the medical professionals whose caring and expertise had kept Izzy with us. I didn't forget them after I won the lottery: for many years after, I made a regular donation to their pediatric cancer ward.

A couple of years ago, the hospital invited me down to Boston to take a look at some of what they had done with the money. I walked in to a fully updated area, including a chemo room for the kids that was painted with bright colors and sports items. It was absolutely cheerful.

All I could think about was my beloved granddaughter, about the long road we walked that resulted in her survival, and the dedication of these wonderful people who had come alongside us to get us through it.

I truly wish they could know Izzy now, so they could see the beauty of the life they saved. Her rough start didn't end with being cured of cancer, though. Because my daughter was quite young when she gave birth to her, Izzy grew up somewhat distant from both of her parents, so I stepped in and became more of a mom to her than a grandmother. She didn't seem to want much financial help, she simply wanted love and encouragement, and sometimes a place to stay. I've always been happy to provide all three.

Izzy goes to college now, always working at least one job and using financial aid to complete her studies. I bought her a home, but she wants to pay it off herself, so I hold the note and function as her bank right now. It's an arrangement that came in handy a few years ago, when a partner of hers tried to lay claim to her property. All I needed to do was threaten to call in the note, and lo and behold, a quitclaim deed appeared almost immediately.

In spite of the satisfaction I felt from saving Izzy's house, I did have a few misgivings about strong-arming the situation that way; however, my granddaughter works hard, is determined to make it on her own, and she didn't deserve to have her home threatened. When she needs something, I'll always have her back.

There are still times when I allow myself to revisit those years of fear and uncertainty as we fought her cancer. As I got older, I started to see a pattern - better said, maybe a continuity - of life, like an interweaving of people and their experiences that leads to a predetermined resolution. I'm so often in awe of the ways in which our individual travels can lead us down dark, dismal roads; then suddenly, what we thought was a hopeless journey opens up to a beautiful vision of God's plan for us.

It was through Izzy's numerous struggles that I first began the process of understanding how God works all things for the good, if we will learn to endure.

Admittedly, my endurance occasionally ran a little low, especially when it came to protecting loved ones against those who, it seemed, were only after the money. I had to intervene more than once to prevent the people I cared about from messy legal matters, stemming from their personal relationships, that had the potential to cost them a great deal.

My method of choice was to make sure that everything was in my name. It worked like a charm. When these relationships ended, and the exes came after the money, they were always disappointed to find out that the people closest to me were legally penniless - and yes, I rather enjoyed their disillusionment. The most satisfying memory of these battles will always be the judge who suggested that the litigant, who was complaining about the fact that I was a filthy rich relative of the plaintiff, would have had a better shot at the money if he had married me.

As the years progressed, I grew exhausted from all of the drama and dilemmas that rode into my life with the lottery money. Sometimes I thought of it like a sideways kind of a curse. I certainly understood, I believe better than most, why it is that the love of money is the root of all evil. It can't buy love, it simply buys things for people you love. That's it.

Money causes changes in people, and worshipping money destroys them. It's as simple as that. I recently heard about an old friend, long gone from my life, who turned obsessed with winning the lottery after I won. Through an unyielding determination to be rich, this person lost everything, including family, friends, and peace of mind.

I can understand why that happened. For me, managing my wealth and the losses that arrived with it was a continuous struggle to stay grounded. There were times that I wanted to give up. Walk away. Maybe go buy an island somewhere, and leave it all behind.

But every time I fell into a place of despair, something would happen that reminded me again of how God turns it all into good.

For example, I think often about my relationship with my brother. Being my only sibling, he and I were all that was left of our nuclear family at the time that I won the lottery.

I couldn't wait to share my good fortune with him, but I also had that same concern with my brother that I had with my own family and friends: I didn't want the money to change us. We had only each other. I was afraid of losing him.

I gifted him as much as I could every year, while keeping it below the maximum that the IRS would allow without making him pay taxes on it. I asked only that he keep an eye on what was done with the money. I requested that he carefully monitor the kids, especially, and make sure it never go toward anything that might be damaging to his family. When I discovered that it was, indeed, being spent that way, I stopped writing him checks. The thought that I might be financing something that was destructive for my brother, his wife, or his children was unbearable to me.

Equally distressing was the fact that as soon as the money stopped, my brother and I became estranged. It was a devastating turn of events. I love my brother and his family, and being cut out of their lives was almost more than I could take. Since the only thing worse than the pain of the estrangement would have been the guilt of paying for things that would hurt them, I stood my ground. In my heart, I feared that I would never see any of them again.

Eventually, I heard that my brother and my niece had gone to their local cable access station and were hosting a program called "The Empty Chair." The setting was a chair with no one in it - just a rose that represented a person who had succumbed to a drug overdose. From that venture, they began an organization called Merrimack Valley Prevention and Substance Abuse Project. To say I was proud to be related to them is a vast understatement, especially as the organization began to grow by leaps and bounds. I was just proud of them from a distance.

Then one day, out of the blue, my brother called me and asked me to join them as a board member, citing my skills in accounting as the reason. Of course, I jumped at the chance. I applied for their 501c3 status, and they were off and running. They were educating families, talking with kids in schools, and providing their services to entire communities. They soon became a regional source, taking their message into Southern New Hampshire.

They held larger events at least once a year to share information on where to get help, how to get help, and the warning signs that someone has a drug problem. My brother is personally on call 24/7 to help anyone in need. He, his wife, and my niece have often attended support groups to help those who have lost loved ones to drugs, and they have advocated for changes and updates in Massachusetts laws that govern drug abuse. At this point, they're receiving grants from various organizations who appreciate their work.

And I got my brother back. Just when I had decided once and for all that it would never be right, that I'd lost more loved ones and they would never return, there it was again: an ugly situation, seemingly hopeless, that turned into something beautiful. Something even more meaningful than it was before, because my respect and admiration for my brother and his family is boundless now.

It occurs to me that I should give them a call and tell them that myself.

As for my children, they both took charge of their lives, choosing to make their own way. They are a constant source of pride for me. It's probably a mother's greatest joy when you realize that you don't just love your kids - you respect them.

After listening to me talk about my shortcomings as a mother, a friend of mine recently asked me what I thought I did *right* as a mother. The question threw me for a loop, because I never before considered the idea that I succeeded in any aspect of motherhood. It's too important a job, the most important one we'll ever do, so I'm always a lot more likely to focus on my mistakes.

If I did anything right, it would be my dedication to parenting by doing. For example, how I kept furthering my education, or how I would always go to church when the kids were young, hoping that they would find their faith through my expression of my own. I wanted to teach them about being charitable, and I think I accomplished that, because they are two of the most loving, generous, compassionate people you'll ever meet.

Perhaps the most significant thing I wanted them to absorb was the importance of being there for family. That's why I eventually sold my beach house and moved back to New Hampshire, where I could be close by in case they or my grandchildren needed me. I doubt that they're aware of this, but my kids have given me a profound sense of reassurance from the fact that in recent years, they have developed a much closer relationship. Parents will know what I mean when I say this: there's something indescribably comforting about knowing that your children will have each other after we're gone.

On the practical side of parenting, Job One for me was to *never* make idle threats. My kids knew that I said what I meant, and more important, I meant what I said. To this day, my son will occasionally comment on the period of time when he was a teenager, hanging out with a group of less-than-virtuous kids, paying no attention to my warning that if I caught them up to no good, I wouldn't hesitate to call the cops on the lot of them. My son included.

That's what I did. Naturally, he wasn't happy with me at the time, but these days he recounts it with a smile on his face and his opinion that I had "guts."

In spite of my own failings, I firmly believe in what they now call "tough love," which in my opinion is no more than putting the quality of your kids' futures above your own need to see them smile. I think women have more trouble with that concept than men do, because we live to see our children happy; however, we've had to take over parenting to a great extent, because there are many men who have abdicated their leadership responsibilities within the family unit.

I know that especially in recent decades, it's become culturally correct to denounce women in general and mothers in particular, yet I don't hear much from the men about their contributions to the problems. When they do speak, it's often about how their rights are being violated, or how unfairly they're being portrayed in the media. Rarely do they comment on their own responsibility for the mess this culture is in.

In my case, I took on most of the leadership duties of our family for years, especially after winning the lottery. I go back and forth a lot on my feelings about that. I think when a mother is in charge of a fully intact family, and has to take over the husband's/father's role while still trying to maintain a maternal relationship with her children, a kind of a split develops. Since the father appears to have minimal power in the home, it's probably natural for the kids to feel sorry for him; conversely, they judge their mother more harshly, especially as she swings back and forth between contrasting roles.

But overall, I'm happy with our outcome. My mom used to say she could go to her grave in peace as long as her family is okay, and I feel the same way. I'm so grateful that I can leave a legacy for my family, one in which they will hopefully do better than I did. I pray for even better lives for my grandchildren, asking God every day to please watch over them. I believe very strongly in the power of prayer, because there were times when I had no power at all except in petitioning God - and He always answered, sometimes right away and in a truly stunning form.

There came a time when I didn't pray a whole lot, though, and it left a deep chasm in my soul.

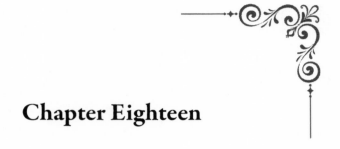

Chapter Eighteen

You would think that with the mountain of blessings I received, I would have had no reason to tumble into a crisis of faith.

I was raised a strict Catholic. I received the Sacraments, attended Mass regularly, and supported my church however I could. As a firm believer in prayer, I would take all my concerns to God and ask for His help. It was something I did pretty much constantly when Izzy was a baby, fighting her cancer, and again when another family member was diagnosed with the disease. He asked me to pray for him, which I did. Constantly. Oddly enough - or perhaps not, when you consider the character of God - the cancer simply went away. It was gone before he had the operation that the doctors had scheduled. They couldn't explain why.

It seemed my petitions were always answered with the best possible outcomes, so prayer was very much a way of life for me. It taught me the key to a strong faith, which I believe is patience.

Yet I was also excessively self-sufficient, which doesn't blend well with faith. I've always been a workaholic, an organizer, a get-it-done type of person. I was the one who kept as much control as I could of both my environment and my feelings about it. I took pride in keeping my emotions intact, regarding myself as the tough gal from Methuen who never fell apart.

It was the perfect setup for falling down. For losing my religion, as the saying goes.

A few years after I won the lottery, during the time right after Bill and I separated - and in spite of my resolution to stay the same person I'd always been - I finally had to acknowledge that I had changed. For the first time in many years, I let my guard down and admitted to myself that I had feelings, and many of them were suddenly quite close to the surface. I was surprised that I would feel wounded more easily than ever before; as a result, the wall I'd built around myself, erected to keep my sanity insulated from the cruel things said to and about me, was beginning to crumble.

After a particularly painful interaction with a loved one, the "why me?" form of guilt started up again. Although I'm not comfortable with exposing the details of this particular situation, I can tell you that it was a direct hit on my self-imposed toughness, one which I hastily masked as a defensive kind of self-pity. After all, it wasn't *my* fault that I couldn't cure the world of hunger, pain, homelessness, ignorance, and anything else that surely, enough money could remedy. Didn't people see the impossibility of my situation? Like the story about the starfish dying on the beach, I wanted to save everyone. I couldn't, but I did save plenty of them, and I wished for others to know that so they would be nicer to me.

Being unaccustomed to allowing myself to feel pain, I think it's obvious that I didn't handle this confrontation well at all.

I tried to turn to my church, but my relationships there had become strained, as well. The people there treated me differently after I won and then made that donation to Saint Monica's. Not everyone was callous or hostile toward me, I don't in any way mean to indicate that; many of them were simply ill at ease, and it showed in our interactions. It made me uncomfortable, too. I often felt separate, like I was on display, and after a while the church no longer seemed like a haven for me.

My defensiveness soon became cynicism, which was a perspective that was totally foreign to me, not to mention exquisitely painful. Nothing will suck the beauty from life like an overriding attitude of sarcasm toward the world. I would have critical thoughts and doubts about others that were laced with bitterness, and I was mistrustful of almost everyone around me.

I tried to keep praying throughout this struggle, and I did find some solace there, but there was a growing distance between me and my faith that wasn't affected by the amount of time I spent on my knees. It was starting to worry me a great deal. The emptiness of that kind of insecurity, where you feel like God is just out of your reach, makes life feel barren.

Then the abuse scandals of the church came to light. It was the final straw. I was initially shocked by the accusations, doing my best to deny them in my own mind, thinking that surely this couldn't happen in a place and a community that beckoned to sinners to come in and find peace with God. It was God's church. His *home*.

As the truth kept emerging, and we were forced to confront the reality of the sickness and the sin in our midst, I was disheartened by the church's response. My son had been an altar boy when he was a child, and while I was grateful and relieved that he wasn't a victim, we personally knew one young man who was. He had been deeply affected by the evil, and the entire debacle turned me away for good. Or so I thought.

I coasted for some time, keeping God in my mind's eye but not talking to Him as much as I once did. I don't know what I was waiting for, or if I was waiting for anything at all; if I had to guess, I would say that I wanted Him to prove to me that He really was in charge. Of course, in doing so, I wanted to then understand why He would allow such hideous things to happen.

Being separated from the church left a terrible, gnawing void in my life, one that I managed to keep on the back burner until the day my dear friend was diagnosed with cancer.

We had been planning a six-week road trip, talking about little else until she told me about the cancer. It was serious: according to the doctors, it was the most severe form of lung cancer that a person could get.

I remember my immediate thought was that I needed to run to God. Then I realized that I'd kind of shut Him out in recent years, and I was afraid He wouldn't want to hear from me.

I was at a complete loss, desperate to find a way to get on God's good side again so He would cure my friend - or at least, so I didn't feel so guilty in asking Him to do so. Being the industrious, self-determining and self-reliant woman that I was, I decided I would strike a bargain with Him: I would go back to church. I would keep going for the rest of my life, if He would just heal her. I would pray like I used to.

I would do anything if He would just save my friend.

No, back then I had no idea how silly I was being. I hurried off to find the local Catholic church, attending the Christmas Eve mass there. I left it feeling more empty than ever before. So I decided to ask God about that - was it because I had been gone for so long, I was rusty? Or was it too late for me to return to the faith?

That last thought shook me to my core. I was scared that God had abandoned me. What I know now is that He was trying to reach me.

Something came to me from out of the blue: *Where is your faith? Where do you place it? In yourself? In a church? Or in your God?*

Well, the answer was obvious, even to me. Faith isn't found in your relationship with any human being or organization. It's the relationship between you and God.

I still wanted to find a church, though. I missed being there, longed for the lightness of spirit I would feel after a service.

There were two other churches in my neighborhood, neither one Catholic, but I decided to pay them a visit. The first one didn't do it for me. They were lovely people, and it was a nice church, but the connection just wasn't there.

The second one, though... That was a match. I drove home afterwards feeling like I'd taken the first step on my way back from a long, sad journey. My friend, in spite of her illness, joked around about it, how it would be a win-win situation for me. Either she would get better, and I would have to keep going to church; or God forbid, she wouldn't get better - but then I wouldn't have to go to church anymore.

I got my sick sense of humor from her. It's her fault.

Shortly thereafter, she went to Boston for a second opinion. They were much more optimistic about her prognosis. Six months after her surgery, she was cleared.

And I'm still in church every Sunday, enjoying the music, absorbing the message, and feeling so much lighter when I leave. As of this writing, my friend and I are getting ready for that six-week road trip we've been looking forward to for so long.

I still retain some of my control-freak ways, but with God at the helm instead of my own sense of independence. Yes, I definitely changed after winning the lottery, but I don't ascribe it to the money. Even though the aftermath brought my emotions to the surface, and the necessity for my growth into sharp relief, the changes were good. I think I might contact David Ropeik, the reporter who followed me around that first year, and tell him he was right - and that maybe, change isn't so bad after all.

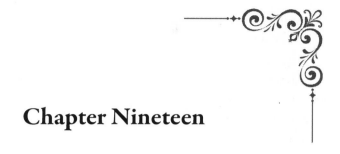

Chapter Nineteen

There's a woman who has been helping me with this memoir, an author who teaches a writing seminar a couple of times a year. I met her when I took her class. She visited me recently at my home, suggesting that I write more about my opinions. She thinks they're interesting.

I pointed out to her that some of my pontificating is already included here, that I wrote about marriage, education, the problems with entitlement, etc. She responded with a strange cackling sound, indicating that I was being a chicken.

"I'm *not* being a chicken," I said. "I just don't want to be boring."

"It's your one and only memoir, Paula. If you ever have the right to be boring, it's now."

Not the most encouraging reply, but I suppose she had a valid point.

Anyway, in the face of my reluctance, she offered to pose some questions to me to help me nudge the creative process. First, she asked me to tell her something that people most often misunderstand about me, and if I could tell them differently, what would I like them to know?

The question itself had me biting my nails, because I'm shy to a fault, and private to the point of being a recluse - which is actually the main reason I'm working with the aforementioned author to begin with.

Most people think I'm outgoing, even an extrovert. I can see why, because I try to present that attitude when I'm out in public, a habit I developed in the aftermath of the win. They're often surprised when I try to tell them that I'm really an introvert, almost phobic about social situations. I'll sit back, smile, listen a lot, and make small talk here and there; but the reality is, I'm way out of my comfort zone in those situations.

Sure, I have no problem standing up in front of an audience and doing a presentation, because that's easy, as long as it's work or a structured presentation and not a social thing. When it comes to venues where I'm expected to schmooze, I have to force myself to interact.

I've hosted many events at my homes throughout the years, but I would be so nervous before a gathering started that there were times when I wanted to cancel it. I hate to admit this: I usually was relieved when last person left, just so I could relax and be myself again. I always told myself that the more I socialized, the easier it would get. It never did.

At my age, I think I can safely assume it will always be something that people don't understand about me. I've actually had some people comment that they think I'm a snob, blaming my demeanor on the fact that I have money, but they couldn't be further from the truth.

The thing is, I've moved well beyond the need to show them differently, which is probably the nicest part of growing older. It's certainly the most freeing.

It's also something that I believe would have happened anyway, regardless of my bank balance. I think about the years of struggling to prove myself to people who were determined to regard me however they chose, or who had already defined my character before ever meeting me, and I regret the amount of time and effort I put into my attempts to change their minds. I would even fret about the opinions of people whom I had never met and probably never would, like the strangers who said such ugly things on public forums like the one in the newspaper after the win. Maybe I was weak, or maybe I just wanted people to approve of me. Perhaps I was trying to remedy the fact that I, too, saw my sudden wealth as something of an injustice, so these people hit that raw nerve inside me; however, they also helped me to finally attain my own peace with myself.

That's one of my concerns about the current climate of incivility in this country, especially the effect social media has on our basic humanity - a point of view that led to the next question.

My author friend asked me what I would want to tell the generations I'll leave behind one day. She wanted to know what my most pressing concerns are, and what I would do about them.

I think social media is at the top of my list. More than its addictive draw, this is a world that is running low on civility, compassion, and dignity, and the anonymity of a message board or the one-way correspondence of a personal page is an efficient vehicle for the destruction of others. It also has the potential, which is realized too often, to create a public persona that bears no resemblance to reality - an effect I believe is every bit as unhealthy as the bullying you see on these sites.

More than anything else, though, I wonder how many hurting people run to a social media source instead of running to God, friends, or family, and wind up looking for the support they need in what they find on a computer screen. I think it further isolates people who already feel alone, and those are the people who worry me the most.

Plus it seems like many people are posting every single moment of their lives, and I think that the more enmeshed we become in the minutiae, the less anyone is listening. Or in this case, reading. And if ever there was a vehicle to cause division, it's the internet. Anyone, anywhere, can be as ugly or as hurtful as they want, and there's not a lot anyone can do to restrain them.

Not that I would necessarily want to, at least not in all situations, but I do wish we could be kinder to each other.

I use social media, but I do so judiciously, sharing certain parts of my life that my friends might find interesting. And yes, like so many moms and grandmas do, I sometimes check in on my kids and grandchildren. Other than that, I keep social media just that: social. I think we'd be better off if we all did that. I can't believe that people would be as cruel as they sometimes are if they had to look directly at the person they wanted to wound.

Then again, that isn't always true. We recently had a situation in Hyannis, Massachusetts, where a woman who was offended by a Donald Trump bumper sticker allegedly plowed her car into the SUV that was bearing it. Social media went insane over it. Some of the comments were grotesque, from both sides; additionally, the new emotional syndrome called "Trump Anxiety Disorder" became more mainstreamed after a local reporter wondered aloud if it would be a successful defense for the accused.

Now I'm in no way a died-in-the-wool Conservative. I'm also not a Liberal, yet lately, I'm nervous when it comes to sharing my political views. Ironically, it seems that all this online free speech is starting to quash free speech.

When I shared that opinion with my friend, she immediately wanted to know about my political persuasion. I declined to answer, so she asked, "Well, do you listen to Talk Radio?"

I do, and I have a couple of favorite hosts, but my go-to shows are the late night ones that talk about weird things, like supernatural events, aliens, and crop circles. It's a guilty pleasure of mine, a respite of sorts from all of the negativity and crazy chaos out there.

I wish it was a better, saner, more tolerant world that we were leaving to the next generation. I also wish we still had our freedoms. If we don't get the government under our control, like it was intended to be, I fear that my children and their children will be regulated to pieces. Case in point: a friend and I went to a favorite restaurant the other day, ordered our cold drinks, and they arrived without straws. When I asked the server about it, she informed us that it was their new policy, because apparently there are now places where straws are banned. No straws unless you ask for them. I mean, we have serious, vital issues that need to be tended to - homelessness, abuse, education, and foreign affairs, just to name a few - and we're worried about *straws*?

It's not that I'm indifferent toward the environment. I care deeply, in more ways than one: I especially care about the *cultural* environment we're handing over to our kids.

Of course, my author friend asked me to expand on that, too.

In essence, I agree with the experts that the breaking down and breaking up of families is the issue at the core of most of our problems. I know that may sound strange, since I'm a divorced woman myself, but that doesn't mean I don't have my misgivings about it; further, I'm of the opinion that divorce itself isn't the main issue within fractured families. It's simply the result.

Marriages break down while they're still marriages. Divorce comes after all of the damage is done, including the negative effects of constant stress and contention on the children. I firmly believe in fighting to keep a marriage together, yet there comes a time when you have to decide if the actual battle is more destructive to the family than ending the war would be. You also have to ask yourself if your limited run here on earth is best spent in a dogged determination to repair something that will simply never work.

Bill and I got along much better after we split for good. We even got to the place of being able to joke sometimes about our parting. He eventually sold the large waterfront house in Salem, preferring to take an apartment instead; in 2016, I sold my beach cottage and bought a small home in Southern New Hampshire so I could be closer to my family.

I finally filed for divorce in the spring of 2018. Bill and I agreed to the settlement with minimal bargaining, so it was wrapped up quickly and quietly.

I remember the day Bill texted me that it was final. Done. Friends had suggested to me that I throw some kind of a celebration when the final decree came through, and I actually played with the idea for a while; but in the moment when I realized that it was over, I felt a melancholy, bittersweet kind of reverence for it. Something important to me, central to my life for decades, was now officially gone. I was legally a total stranger to the man I had married, the father of my children. Perhaps because we had been apart for so long, I was able to look at that text and in my heart, wish him every good thing that life could bring his way.

Like I told my author friend, it didn't strike me as a moment to throw a party.

She asked me how my faith lined up with my divorce. "After all," she pointed out, "God hates divorce, right?"

I agreed with her. God does hate divorce. We *all* hate it. Without exception, it's a tragedy. But it happens, and when it does, even God makes provisions for it.

She asked me if the road trip I had recently taken with a few friends had anything to do with getting away after the divorce. At first, I said it didn't, because we'd planned it for such a long time; then I realized that even though the idea of an epic cross-country jaunt was a long-held dream, having it come true so close to the final decree did help me to adjust to the reality of my new single status.

"You surprise me," she said. "A lot, actually."

"Why?"

"You never give the answers I expect."

She was packing her supplies into the gargantuan bag she carries everywhere, shaking her head like she was deep in thought.

I asked her what she was thinking, and when she turned to look at me, I could see another question forming. It makes me nervous when she does that, because it means that she's about to push me into uncomfortable waters again.

She hoisted her bag onto her shoulder and said, "I think you should write about the fact that very few people know the real you. By the way, is there anyone who does?"

I nodded. "One person."

Her name is Doti.

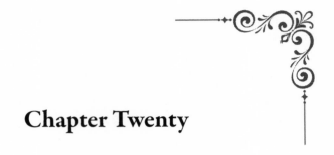

Chapter Twenty

Doti is my best friend.

I look at that sentence, and I realize it comes nowhere near the truth of our relationship. Doti is so much more than a best friend: she's the sister I thought I would never have.

She's a bit of a free spirit, in contrast to my "waste not, want not" way of living. She's the kind who would throw open the windows to feel the intensity of a storm while I would be battening down the hatches. Doti has a joyous, irreverent sense of humor that tempers my propensity to be somber. Everything about the two of us together is wonderfully unique, beginning with the day we met.

I lived in Salisbury at the time, and the local politics were getting out of hand, functioning within the good ol' boy system that was populated by politicians who never seemed to have anyone running against them. Now I'm not at all a politician - I always left that kind of thing to others - but after several discussions with my brother, he got tired of listening to me complain and talked me into running for office.

I was sure I couldn't beat the system that was already in place, but I figured I might give the powers-that-were a little competition. Or at least a mild headache, if nothing else. It was my goal to maybe wake them up a bit.

In order to get onto the ballot, I had to file a petition with fifteen signatures from registered voters in Salisbury. I took the petition with me to the senior bowling league I had just joined in Amesbury, but I didn't know anybody very well yet, so I asked if anyone there was from

Salisbury. Most of the ladies were from Amesbury or Merrimack, but one of them pointed me to this small, smiling, pixie-ish woman across the room.

"That's Doti," she said. "She's a nice lady, from your neck of the woods, and she'll probably sign for you."

I went over to her, introduced myself, told her why I was there, and she signed my paperwork. We became friendly after that.

Doti used to go out for a meal after bowling, and she started asking me to join her and her friends. She has such a wonderful way about her, a warm, welcoming attitude that instantly put me at ease. It felt good to be included, to be accepted into her circle and be part of a nice group. The more I got to know her, the more I liked her.

Eventually, I started inviting her to join me in some of my own interests. I told her I was a volunteer at the senior center, then asked her if she would like to volunteer with me. She did, and ended up being the Monday Bingo caller.

I was also involved with doing taxes via the AARP/IRS, pro bono, for seniors. I asked Doti if she'd like to be involved with that and to my surprise, she said she would, so I dragged her along out to Salem State for our week of certification. Then we spent the next few years doing taxes at the Salisbury, Amesbury, and Merrimack senior centers. I'd never met anyone so dedicated, dependable, and easy-going.

Our friendship was growing. Doti, too, has a passion for Bingo, and we would go play together on Tuesdays, kidding around about competing with each other for the jackpot.

I invited her to fly out to Las Vegas with me so she could experience a *real* Bingo game, if you know what I mean. She insisted on paying for her own flight, but I still had the house in Vegas, so at least she let me provide that for her. We took one other friend with us and had the time of our lives.

The following year, Doti and I went out to Las Vegas again for a "Mega Bingo" event. Again, we had a blast. I'd never felt so comfortable with any other friend.

I used to host an annual clambake for the people closest to me, and she was always on top of my invitation list. At our bowling league, Doti and I arranged it so we were always together on the same team; and although we didn't pay attention to it at the time, we were becoming like family - it was as if we'd known each other forever. By now, she could actually finish my sentences. I could read her mood with one look. I don't remember when, but it occurred to me one day that for the first time in my life, I had an honest-to-goodness best friend.

We can have many friends in life, such as good neighbors or coworkers, and I've had a few of them - but my definition of a best friend is Doti. She is one who I tell my deepest thoughts to. I share my feelings and everything I think with her, and I know she'll never tell a soul. I could never say that about anyone else I have ever met and called a friend. I've been hurt many times by telling people whom I trusted something that I later regretted sharing with them, but never once did Doti betray me.

While I say it's the best relationship of my life, I have to wonder if Doti sometimes has her doubts about that, because I've been dragging the poor woman into my own projects for ten years now. We joke about that a lot, but the truth is, she says she has loved every minute.

We decided we would take a cross-country trip with a couple of other ladies, planning it for May of 2018. We would rent one of those big travel vans and go wherever the road took us. There were places we'd never seen, adventures we'd never taken. We called them our "bucket list," after the popular expression for daydreams about the things we want to do in life.

My friend Danielle and I had been talking about it for years, even before I met Doti, planning it as a congratulatory celebration for after we retired. Danielle was the last one of us to make it to retirement, in 2017, so we chose May of 2018 for our departure.

Doti had never done much traveling. She hadn't been many places at all, which made it even more exciting for all of us. I had the entire trip worked out in my head: I would rent the RV, which of course was going to be the biggest cost. We all would share the costs of gas, tolls, and other expenses. We'd be staying mostly in hotels, as none of us are seasoned campers; however, since sleeping in the great outdoors for a night was on the bucket list - don't ask me why - we did plan on camping out in the Grand Canyon.

What I didn't plan on was Doti getting very sick. The friend I mentioned earlier, the one who was diagnosed with cancer, was Doti. It happened in the autumn of 2017.

After the initial shock of it, and with praying harder than I had since Izzy was a baby, we set about getting her cured. Although I probably shouldn't have been - knowing Doti like I do - I was flabbergasted by her concern over missing our road trip. She was determined to go. And go, we did, with the added joy of Doti being cured.

Part Three: May, 2018 -
The Road Trip

We had planned to hit the road on May 1st, but there were a few issues with the van we were renting, so we had to pick it up later than expected. It was bigger than I remembered it being when I had reserved it, and that was a little distracting; but I was use to driving long vans, so I didn't do too badly bringing it from the place in Maine where we rented it, back to my home. I was glad Doti came with me, though. She kept me centered throughout a very long day.

Because of the late hour when we got home, we decided to head out on our trip the next day, May 2nd. Doti spent the night at my house and Kate - another friend who was joining us - met us there at 7:00 a.m. Then we headed down to Methuen to pick Danielle up.

We decided to go to Dunkin Donuts before we headed out. It was the backdrop for our first incident.

As we were leaving the restaurant, all of a sudden, Doti was panicking. She couldn't find her pocketbook with her money, charge cards, passport, etc. Basically, her entire life was in her purse.

I remember thinking, *Well, this is a good start*.

We frantically searched every place where we had drawn a breath. We scoured the RV, ran back inside the restaurant and checked the counter - and under it - and asked if anyone had seen it.

Lo and behold, it was waiting right on the table where we had just sat and eaten, sitting there completely untouched.

I briefly considered zip-tying it to Doti's arm. That would be the first of what would be countless laughs on our epic, well-planned, bucket list of a road trip.

Our first stop was Hershey, PA. It's a charming city, known of course for its chocolate, the aroma of which is everywhere. They also have a butterfly atrium and a rose garden. I had heard that they have Hershey Kisses street lights; sure enough, they did, and they were amazing. So creative and fun.

We toured the town, stopping to take several pictures of the four of us - plus Patrick, my New England Patriots teddy bear that accompanied us on the trip, sort of like our mascot. We called ourselves "Patrick's Angels." He's in almost all of the pictures and videos we took throughout.

After a pleasant afternoon in Hershey, we headed off to Pennsylvania Dutch Country, where we would be staying our first night. We were famished by the time we got there, so I asked the hotel desk clerk about any places to eat. He referred me to a place close by called Good 'N' Plenty.

As soon as I pulled into the restaurant's parking lot, I had a strong déjà vu moment: years earlier, when I owned the travel agency and offered motor coach tours, we spent a few days in Pennsylvania Dutch country. The restaurant we'd just pulled up to was the same one that I'd brought my clients to for dinner. Everything was home made, with the "family style" type of service where you sit in groups at big tables covered with old-fashioned checkered tablecloths, sharing a variety of appetizers, entrees, and desserts with the other diners. Of course, Patrick the Patriot Bear posed for pictures with everyone. It was so much fun that throughout the rest of our trip, Danielle kept whining that she wanted to go back there. Me, too. I wanted to go back for the stroganoff and the Shoo-fly Pie.

But eventually, we had to tear ourselves away and take off for Harpers Ferry, West Virginia, which was on our way to Colonial

Williamsburg. At this point I was doing all the driving, even though we had planned for Doti to share it with me. With our late start on the road, she hadn't yet had the opportunity to test out the RV, and the manual strongly suggested that anyone planning to drive it needed to practice before doing so.

After touring Williamsburg for a few hours, Doti and I left Kate and Danielle to do some sightseeing while we found a nice, roomy parking lot where Doti could practice driving the RV. I found myself reflexively almost putting my foot through the floor with my shadow-braking, but she did a surprisingly good job. I felt comfortable and very relieved that the next day she could start sharing the driving.

Along the way we saw a sign for Gettysburg, and I just had to stop. I went on and on about it, telling my travel companions that I had been there before, explaining to them how it was where George Washington and his men once stayed. I felt like an expert on the subject; however, when we got there, I was showing off my expertise to one of the people at the information area - and he let me know that Gettysburg was during the Civil War. What I was talking about was during the *Revolutionary* War.

Yes, I was embarrassed. But hey, I was only about a hundred years off on my dates - a fact that the girls found quite humorous.

Colonial Williamsburg was a phenomenal experience. We wandered the streets and the beautiful gardens, and took a tour of the historic area that they call the "Ghost Walk." Our guide told us stories about spirits who, legend has it, still live in Williamsburg. I left with the impression that perhaps they do. The feeling I had, one that I could only describe as a sense of the past, was overwhelming. Gettysburg was one of my favorite stops.

It was hard to leave, actually. There was so much more to see, but we had to hit the road again. We were stopping in North Carolina for a few hours to see my granddaughter. While I thought it was tough to leave Gettysburg, it was ten times more difficult to get back in the RV after seeing my beloved Izzy. The time went by way too fast.

By evening, we were heading toward Tennessee, anxious to find out if the Smoky Mountains really did look like smoke. Knowing we wouldn't make it there, not with as late as it was getting, we decided to stop for a quick bite to eat and just stay in North Carolina for the night.

We were almost all the way to the state's western border when we wound up behind an oil truck. There was a very strong odor coming from the truck, like fumes of some sort. Doti noticed that the gas tank cover was off and just hanging, and suggested that I get alongside of the cab so we could signal the driver, so I did. I assumed she would roll down her window and call out to him... But this is Doti we're talking about.

Instead of rolling down her window to tell him, she looked at him through her closed window, waiting for him to notice her - and then she held her nose. She pinched her nostrils shut and stared at him like she was telling him that he stank or something.

Naturally, he didn't appreciate that. It was my first experience with the highway form of road rage: he crowded me for a while, yelling something we couldn't hear and really didn't want to anyway, with the only saving grace being that he had to turn off at the next exit.

Understanding that Doti wasn't exactly an expert at American Sign Language, I told her she was never allowed to converse with her hands again. Ever. Then I switched places with her so she could keep her hands on the wheel.

I would have kept yelling at her, but I was distracted, noticing that the scenery seemed very familiar. I realized that a few years back, I had been there for my granddaughter's wedding, held in the same North Carolina mountains that we were now driving through.

Then I saw the sign for Fatz.

The way I was suddenly pointing, demanding that Doti pull over into their parking lot, scared the dickens out of her. I guess she thought it was an emergency, and in a way, it was: Fatz has the best Calabash Chicken on the planet. And biscuits to die for. Not to mention, homemade peach cobbler and double chocolate cake. We stopped for one of our best and biggest meals of the trip before we settled in for the night.

We arrived in Tennessee the next day. I was thrilled by the fact that the Smoky Mountains really *do* look smoky, and even more excited that we would knock three more items off of my bucket list: The Grand Ole Opry, the Johnny Cash Museum, and Dollywood. All were truly amazing, and we had a blast, but they didn't make the top of my "Road Trip Favorite Stories" list. Not after we got to Memphis.

In an RV as large as the one we were traveling in, parking can be an issue, since lots of hotels have enclosed parking. Driving around, we happened upon a nice young man who works for the Tennessee Titans. Now if you're a Patriots fan, or a Titans fan for that matter, you know about the intense rivalry between the two teams. Yet even after meeting Patrick the Patriot Bear, this generous man invited us to park our van in the Titans' parking lot. It almost made me feel bad that we so thoroughly trounced them in the playoffs. Not quite, but it came close.

I will give them this, though: Titans Stadium is absolutely stunning.

After a day at Graceland, which we decided was even better than we'd heard it would be, we were off to Louisiana. Specifically, we were heading for New Orleans. While en route, we found a hotel with an open area that would accommodate the RV, yet it was only three blocks from the French quarter.

What an incredible city. We spent three days there, having the time of our lives. We took a cruise down the Mississippi, went to many of the countless places to shop, and visited a casino on the waterfront. I also got my first taste of authentic Cajun food, which I'm sorry to say, I wasn't a fan of.

The vistas on the trip west to Texas, via Route 10 from New Orleans, were like watching paint dry. There wasn't much to see except what they call "sand devils," the sand storms that seem to rise up out of nowhere like miniature white tornados. We did go to the Alamo, which I'd anticipated being be the highlight of our time there. It was the 300th anniversary of its inception, and looking at the structure that was still standing three centuries later was enough to bring a lump to my throat; however, the San Antonio Riverwalk was easily the best part of the visit. We took a cruise down the San Antonio River, stopped at the shops and restaurants, and were simply in awe of the whole experience. They call it "The American Venice" for good reason.

By this time I thought we'd all be wearing out. We had traveled across several states, visiting all of our planned stops as well as many unplanned diversions, but we were somehow even more eager to hit the highway. There is something magical about driving the wide-open road that stretches out in front of you, and then finding towns and people - all unique, yet connected by an American identity - at the end of each one. It's energizing. And humbling.

So we made our way through New Mexico, heading to Arizona to see Tombstone. The scenery on the way was awe-inspiring, but the signs that warned us about rattlesnakes... Not so much, especially for Danielle. Sure, we have snakes in New England, but not in great enough numbers that you find "Beware Of Rattlers" signs posted in your average parking lot. It freaked her out. I must admit, I was looking down at my feet a little more often, just in case.

We had meticulously planned a night of camping in the Grand Canyon, right down to our menu, except for the fact that we forgot the essential condiments for the hot dogs. So Danielle, trooper that she is, would pick up packets of mustard, ketchup, relish, and even a packet of onions at our various stops along the way. With that, we were totally prepared. But after the rattlesnake warnings, I could sense that the three of them had lost their enthusiasm for sleeping in the great outdoors.

I was right. They didn't want to camp out. Even after I teased them about being babies, they flat out refused. I felt like I'd been voted off the island or something, and we never did camp in the Grand Canyon.

Only Doti seemed to regret it later. To be honest, I think I would have hated it anyway. It was just something I wanted to cross off my list.

We did take the canyon tour, though. Doti and I went out on the glass walkway that hangs out for miles over the canyon - definitely not a place for anyone who may be an acrophobic, but Doti was thrilled with it. I had already been there a few times, so even though I knew what to expect, I enjoyed seeing it through her eyes. Danielle and Kate didn't go with us, the big chickens.

We then went to Las Vegas, staying at my favorite casino, so we could indulge in a Bingo binge. Probably because I'm so familiar with Las Vegas, the best part of that stop for me was when we found a laundromat. Living with three other women in small quarters, with only one duffel bag of clothes to last for six weeks, meant that clean laundry was a real treat.

From Vegas we headed to California. I always wanted to take the road from Vegas to California, and I wasn't disappointed. It was some of the most exquisite scenery I have ever seen. We stayed in Fresno for one night, which was a surprisingly unremarkable city, then went on to San Francisco.

I'd been there before, but it was nothing like this time, probably because I was now seeing it with beloved friends. We did it all: The Golden Gate Bridge, Alcatraz, Pier 39, and we took the trolley - and we visited Haight-Ashbury, which is well worth the trip all by itself. It's known as the birthplace of the 1960's counterculture movement, so the history - even just the aura there - is fascinating.

This leg of our trip was a first for Danielle and Doti, and I fully enjoyed their wide-eyed appreciation of the beautiful area we were in. It was originally an item on Danielle's bucket list, but I thought San Francisco was easily one of the best stops of the trip.

Everything was going so well. I remember thinking that all things considered, we'd had a relatively trouble-free road trip. I should have known better.

Our last night in San Francisco, Doti was going to follow me down the street in the van so I could return our rental car. Just a small detail - except when my beloved Doti is involved, small details can become big deals.

To this day, I don't know where her head was at; but as she backed the big RV out, she came too close to the carport of the hotel. Actually, she hit it. Instead of stopping, she tried to clear it, and she sort of smooshed the top of the RV.

I remember my feeling of incredible helplessness, not to mention disbelief, as I watched her skin the top of that van.

My first thought was one of gratitude for the added insurance I'd purchased with the rental. My second was trying to recall what my deductable was. Third, I wondered how far I could throw her.

Not really, but I did intend to yell at her. Or at least act like I was mad for a while, which I tried to do. But I just can't stay angry with Doti.

On second thought...

I don't know exactly what happened to her, but as I turned into the car rental place, I guess she must have kept going straight. I hurriedly reached into my pocket for my cell phone so I could tell her to come back. It wasn't there. I figured I left it in the hotel room.

So all I could do was hang out by myself on the street, looking for little Doti's head peeking through the massive RV's windshield. After fifteen minutes or so, I spotted her slowly, carefully approaching, and I started waving my arms and yelling at her to pull over.

I have to wonder what my expression looked like as I watched her drive slowly, carefully past me.

She totally missed me. Don't ask me how, because you won't find scads of sandal-clad grandmothers claiming San Francisco street corners, trying desperately to hail an RV. Maybe in Vegas, but not in Frisco. And the street was pretty much empty, so I wasn't exactly blending into a crowd.

Anyway, she finally came back and turned into the car rental's parking area. I took off immediately, running after her - picturing myself doing a Bruce Willis move and leaping onto the back, holding on for dear life while she puttered around the parking lot.

Once I was safely ensconced in the passenger's seat, I had to stifle an impulse to scream at her. Then she got that look on her face, the one that says, "I'm so sorry. Please don't be mad at me. I love you." It's an expression so innocent, so endearing, all you can do is sigh and tell her all's well.

By the way, my cell phone wasn't at the hotel. We did a location search on my laptop, and found it inside the rental car we'd just returned. It was small comfort to know that at least it was locked up tight in there. I'm *very* conscientious about locking things up, after all. Very responsible.

So we had to change our plans of getting up extra early and hitting the highway, since they didn't open until 9:00 a.m. We were there at 8:50, and they were kind enough to open car up for me.

Finally, we were back on the road, driving up the California coast to Seattle. Oregon was just lovely, so green and uniquely beautiful that I regretted not scheduling a day there, but we were heading to Seattle drop Kate off. She would be staying with family, then flying home later.

We stayed over in Seattle, resting up for one of the places I was most looking forward to: Canada. We were going to take the ferry into Victoria, British Columbia. I'd been there before, but Doti and Danielle hadn't. I couldn't wait to show it off to them, since it's one of my favorite places on earth.

The problem in Victoria was, again, that we couldn't find a hotel with outdoor parking for the RV. After four hours of searching without finding a place to stay - and with Danielle getting so bored that she was snapping pictures of a horse's behind for laughs - we headed out to where we would catch the ferry out of Victoria the next morning. By this time it was about 9:00 p.m. and I just wanted to sleep.

I saw a small airport that had a parking area, so I drove in, paid the twelve dollar fee, and we decided to sleep there. We figured we could head to the ferry the next morning.

The van, though, took up three spots. Never one to leave well enough alone, I felt guilty, so I decided I was going to pay for two more spots. As I was heading to the machine to purchase them, a security guard came out. When I explained what I was doing, and how I was looking forward to sleep, he said we were not allowed to sleep there and we had to leave, then suggested that we park at the ferry waiting area instead.

I was stunned. Surely he couldn't turn away three exhausted seniors in their time of need.

He could, and he did.

All those hours of searching for someplace to grab a few hours of sleep, and we wound up getting booted from an airport parking lot. I couldn't even blame Doti for the screw up this time. After all, we'd agreed to wing it. We had all been so excited about spending the rest of our road trip flying by the seat of our pants. Going where the wind blew us. Oh, the *romance* of it, you know?

As I pulled away from the airport, I would have traded all of that romance for a hot shower and a cot.

We took the man's advice, and needless to say, we didn't sleep much in the RV. I had been driving all day, so I was plenty cranky. Doti and Danielle had been riding all day, so they were, as well, and we did do a little bickering. I think I arrived at a new level of crabby when I announced that no one was allowed to use the porta toilet in the RV for anything but peeing. Nothing else. Close quarters and all.

Doti slept in driver's seat, Danielle took the passenger seat, and I laid down on the couch. We had a bed in the back, but it had a ton of stuff on it and we were too tired to clean it off.

It was so quiet that just the ticking of the clock kept me awake. It was driving me crazy. Danielle, bless her, solved that problem by taking the battery out, after which I was quickly dozing off.

That's when they both started snoring. I tried to ignore it, I counted sheep, I covered my ears, and then I screamed, "*Shut up!*"

They did, like a light switch being flipped. Finally, I was drifting off again - but that was when Danielle decided that she had to have the bed after all. She came stumbling to the back, bumping into things, making just enough noise to keep me awake as she moved the pile of stuff off the bed. I didn't yell at her. I think I'd lost all hope by that time.

At our next stop, I saved our friendship by buying a pair of heavy-duty earplugs. When we crossed the border back into the United States, I almost got out of the van to kiss the ground.

Montana and Wyoming were gorgeous. The unrestricted views of Big Sky country, with the sky stretching out into its infinity, reminded me of looking at the ocean.

We saw all of the expected tourist attractions, like Old Faithful, which was so stunning it brought tears to my eyes, and Glacier National Park. We had much more fun back in the U.S. than we did in Canada, especially when we found a Bingo hall at one of the nearby casinos. By the time we left, we were excited again about our trip. We were heading next to the Dakotas, because the Badlands were another item on Doti's bucket list, and Danielle and I wanted to see that area, too.

After visiting Mount Rushmore, which I thought was actually a little disappointing, I took over the driving to the Badlands. Doti got confused and gave me the wrong directions, landing us in the middle of nowhere. I mean, there was *nothing* around. It was isolated. And it was scary. Just as we realized we were lost, some warning lights appeared on the RV's dash, telling me there was something wrong with the tires at the same moment that the GPS ordered me to correct our mistake by turning onto a small dirt road.

I was already tired and getting pretty anxious, thinking it would be safer to stick to paved road in case we got stranded or something by the bad tires, and wouldn't you know it - we ended up right in the middle of the Badlands.

Thankfully, we found the greatest little shop in the friendliest small town of the entire trip. There was a hotel there, but it was booked, so the owners told us about Wall Drug Store. It was several miles away, yet they insisted that it was our best chance at finding someplace to stay.

As we took off, it was time to cue my whining:

"I'm nervous about the tires, we're all starving, the sun is setting, and we're in the middle of the Badlands."

It occurred to me that I was having a Blues Brothers moment, for sure. I was just waiting for one of my companions to say, "And we're wearing sunglasses."

At this point I was mad, I was pouting, and I didn't want to talk to *anybody*. I had no intention of ever being in a good mood again. I wanted to drive straight ahead until we hit civilization, barely taking note of the beauty of the Badlands sunset.

After several minutes of stony silence, Doti finally mumbled, "Well... You can mark Badlands off your bucket list now, at least."

"It wasn't on *my* bucket list," I snapped.

"Yeah, but it was on *mine*."

She had that "I'm sorry" expression again, and suddenly, we burst out laughing. I gave her hell for getting me out of my pouty mood. I'd wanted to stay angry, and she screwed that up for me. No one but Doti has ever been able to do that.

I didn't bother being upset for the rest of our trip. With Doti there, being mad is always a waste of time.

Wall Drug Store was a ton of fun. Turns out it's a very popular tourist attraction, a place that built its welcoming reputation by the simple gesture of offering free ice water to travelers. With hot coffee at only five cents per cup, it was definitely one of our favorite stops. They had a hotel there, a restaurant, and of course a lovely shop. Their goal is to rejuvenate weary travelers, and they do it to perfection.

Afterwards, we agreed that it was time to head for home, but we decided to go via Atlantic City so we could play a little Bingo and get spa treatments.

It was definitely the epic road trip we'd hoped for, especially because of the blunders and gaffes that we didn't expect. The die-hard planner in me, always trying to anticipate every contingency, had to learn to smile at those interruptions while we solved them. Doti made sure I learned the lesson well, bless her heart.

What I'll remember most of all is the laughter. I don't think of myself as someone with a great sense of humor, but Doti has always had a way of making me laugh until I cry.

Lately, though, I cry for other reasons.

August 2018

Even though Doti and I were already best friends before the road trip, we became even closer afterwards.

I had a surgery planned for when I got home, a reconstruction of my left foot. I knew I'd be unable to walk for ten weeks. Doti had a similar procedure done years ago, so she knew what I'd be going through.

Remember, I like to think of myself as a superwoman; however, I knew I needed to have someone bring me home after surgery. I thought I could manage from there, that I didn't need anyone to stay with me.

Doti disagreed. She brought me home and then refused to leave.

Good thing, too, because I discovered almost immediately that I was wrong about not needing her. I had one disaster after another the first three days after surgery, and Doti was right there to come to my aid. For the first time in my life, I had to accept help from someone. The surprise to me was that eventually, I realized that it wasn't that bad. I could need, and I could accept someone meeting that need.

So after she cared for me, helping me with everything and letting me know what to expect with my foot, she told me we needed to talk.

She explained that while she'd gotten a clean bill of health before our trip - no lung cancer - she'd been experiencing some double vision and numbness in her mouth.

Doti has Stage IV brain cancer. It's inoperable. She has maybe a year or less to live.

She said she would need aggressive radiation treatment. It won't cure her, because there is no cure, but it will relieve some of the swelling of the tumor that is causing her issues.

I had this frantic feeling of helplessness, casting about in my mind to find a way to undo this. I simply couldn't accept it. Alone in my room that night, I prayed, I cried, and I prayed some more. Then I looked for someone, something to blame - maybe me. Maybe I shouldn't have taken her on that road trip. Maybe it affected her illness.

I've come to understand that the mental machinations we go through after a loss, or one that is impending, are a blocking device of sorts. They help us to avoid the reality until we're able to accept it.

I knew I needed to accept it fast, because now, Doti needed me. But I had no idea what to do. How to help her. There were no plans that I could make, because there was no possible way to predict the next year of life with her. There was no schedule, no checklist, no road map to follow.

Then I thought about Doti, how she lived her life without a checklist. She isn't fond of schedules. She uses no road map - and that was how we wound up in beautiful places that I never would have found without her.

With that, I had my plan, which was to have no plan at all. I would follow her lead, and be the kind of friend to Doti that she always was to me.

I'm trying to be strong for her, but we still horse around, we laugh, and I'll enjoy every second I get to spend with her. She is my once-in-a-lifetime friend, my best friend, and I'm a far better person for having her in my life. I'm also far from being the only person who can say that.

You can have all the money in the world, but the only thing we can take with us, and the only mark we leave behind, is the love that we give to others. Doti has left a truly unique, beautiful, sweeping impression that will live on in the souls of everyone she ever touched. Especially me.

Sure, money helped get her finances in order, giving her some peace of mind. It helped to take her on a trip of a lifetime. But when she's gone, and I wake up to all of the days that follow without her, I'll remember how meaningless those pieces of paper that buy us things really are.

Then I'll remember Doti, and I'll thank her for letting me bask in the light that shines from her soul. And I'll always thank God for the immense riches she brought to my life.

September 2018

My author friend was here again today. She sat on the floor like she always does, and we chatted for a while after we reviewed the manuscript.

I noticed her tapping her pen on the floor, a sign that she's not quite satisfied with our efforts, so I asked her about it.

She answered with, "What have you learned about yourself over the past twenty years?"

Like I said, she tends to push me out of my comfort zone. I had to think about it for a while.

I learned that there are parts of my personality that I really do like, once I realized that I *had* a personality, something that I thank Doti for showing me. I have a sense of humor, a soft spot for the elderly, and I rail against bullies. I squeal like a little kid when I win Bingo, and I would do anything for the people I love - even if that means allowing them to hate me.

It took a while, but I learned to roll with the punches in life, especially the comments, insults, and innuendos after I won the lottery. I smile, I'm polite, and then I simply walk away and ignore them. I've saved a lot of time that way.

She also asked me how I hope to be remembered. That one was a little easier to answer. I want the loved ones I leave behind to know that there were many good things I did when no one was watching and that no one knows about. I want them to do the same in their lives.

"Is that your legacy, then?" she asked.

"No. I hope that's a couple of things, really. I hope I inspired people to give of themselves. To help others out, especially when they don't even ask for help, and to be outside of their own heads enough that they are alert to others' needs. Second, I want them to honor the importance of family. When my granddaughter got cancer, reality struck. I realized then how important family is, and I took a hard look at where my priorities were."

I thought about it for another minute, then I added, "And don't forget to tell those most precious to you, 'I love you.' Three little words that can change an entire life."

She opened her computer then and brought up a 2017 Chronicle feature, where the reporter came to my little house in New Hampshire to catch up with me twenty years after the win. We watched it together, and I noticed that my friend was smiling at the end.

"How was it, writing your memoir?"

I had to laugh. "It was like reading my own diary for the first time. I definitely got to know myself better."

"Seems to me that even after everything that's happened, you're still just Paula," she said.

"I suppose. I went from the working class poor who didn't fit in to the millionaire who didn't fit in."

"So, where are you now?"

"What do you mean, 'where am I now?'" I looked around. I was in my home, reclining with my foot up on the arm of my easy chair.

"In your head. Are you holding up okay, with everything that's going on?"

I nodded. "The foot's healing well."

"But how's about your heart?"

"That will take a lot more time," I said.

Actually, I doubt that any amount of time will heal the loss of Doti, but I'll do my best to go on. I'll live the life of an average retired woman, busy myself with outside interests and hobbies, and continue my charitable efforts while I grow old. And I think I'll be fine with that, by the way - becoming an old woman, I mean. The way I look at it, even though we lose our hearing and our vision fades, all of the important things become so much clearer.

I suppose I did change in some ways. I'm more spontaneous now, and free of many of the burdens that weighed me down for so long - including those checks. My life is much freer without them; and although I'm indescribably grateful for the life I was able to build with the money, I'm even more thankful for the help I was able to give others. Those people touched me deeply, and they will remain in my heart forever.

But the core of my soul stayed the same. I'm still just Paula: Mom, grandmother, retired accountant, senior citizen. Lover of Bingo.

It's been a very rich life, indeed.

Made in the USA
Columbia, SC
04 October 2018